RECKONING WITH RACE

RECKONING WITH RACE

AN UNFINISHED JOURNEY

FREDERICK ALLEN

FOREWORD BY ANDREW YOUNG

Forefront
BOOKS

Photos courtesy of the *Atlanta Journal-Constitution*: Martin Luther King Sr. (page 1); George Wallace & Marvin Griffin, Roy Harris (page 2); Maynard Jackson, Atlanta Child Murders search party (page 3); Wayne Williams, Lewis Slaton (page 4); Coretta Scott King & Ralph Abernathy, Hosea Williams (page 5); Julian Bond & John Lewis, Bond & Rosa Parks (page 6); Carl Sanders (page 8); Freaknik (page 12); protesters (page 15).

Lafayette Square Photo Credit: Getty / *The Washington Post*

Published by Forefront Books.
Distributed by Simon & Schuster.

Library of Congress Control Number: 2022920450

Print ISBN: 978-1-63763-152-2
E-book ISBN: 978-1-63763-153-9
Cover Design by Bruce Gore, Gore Studio, Inc.
Interior Design by PerfecType, Nashville, TN

This book is dedicated in loving memory to Rebecca Logan.

CONTENTS

FOREWORD
by Andrew Young

Back in 1982, when I was mayor of Atlanta, Rick Allen came by my office at city hall one day to ask a favor. He was taking a year off from his job as political columnist for the *Atlanta Journal-Constitution* to go on an international trip with his wife, Linda. He asked me if I would write a letter of introduction for him to use in foreign ports of call. I told him I'd be happy to. He returned that afternoon and picked up an envelope with a letter I'd written that began, "To Whom It May Concern: The bearer of this letter is an enemy of freedom-loving peoples everywhere and should be arrested on sight." The look on his face was priceless! Then he found the second envelope underneath, with a proper diplomatic greeting, and heaved a big sigh of relief.

I tell that story for several reasons. First, I was fond enough of Rick to play a practical joke on him and be pretty sure he'd take it well. More important, I admired the sense of adventure that sent Rick and Linda on their journey. I had dinner with them in London a few months later and they were obviously broadening their horizons. Last, Rick has an openness to new ideas and different ways of thinking that have served him well in his career as a journalist, author, TV commentator, historian, and now in this book that chronicles his journey of learning about race and racism.

As Rick will be the first to tell you, he is not a civil rights activist. He is an observer with a sense of fairness and a willingness to look at things through the eyes of others. His career spans a half century, from the early 1970s, when he covered the election of Maynard Jackson as the first African American mayor of Atlanta, to now, with raw divisions testing our nation in the aftermath of George Floyd's murder and Donald Trump's presidency. Rick has told me he fears he may have been slow to recognize some of the chronic, unresolved issues that continue to hinder racial equality and healing in our society; I told him he was not alone in that. We've lived through wrenching times that have forced us all to learn more, think harder, and see more clearly. I reminded him that during the most trying days of the civil rights movement, Martin Luther King Jr. would turn to me in places like Birmingham, Alabama, and say, "Let's find some white folks we can talk to." Rick is White folks we can talk to.

I think two key moments in his newspaper career illustrate Rick's growth on matters of race. In 1975, during Mayor Jackson's first term in office, the *Atlanta Constitution* ran a series called "City in Crisis" that lamented the end of White political control in Atlanta. Rick was part of the team who wrote the series. In this memoir Rick shares his regret for his role in reporting stories he now calls "one-sided, deaf to the voices of the Black community, and highly unsettling to many in the city." I'd have to say he's right about that.

The second key moment came a dozen years later, in 1987, when Rick came to my defense during another period when his newspaper was embroiled in an ugly episode that involved me. He covers the details in the chapter "Julian Bond and John Lewis"— how the *Atlanta Journal-Constitution* repeated unfounded accusations against me, how the sources Rick had cultivated over the years exonerated me, and how he resigned in protest when his editors declined to report what he'd learned, which turned out to be absolutely accurate. Rick had come a long way in his dealings with Black leaders. Needless to say, I appreciated what he did, and I was glad when he went directly to CNN to be their national political analyst.

Rick has also shared with me a concern that his book may not offer much in the way of insights for Black readers, or worse, that it may revisit painful issues that we would rather not rehash. He has learned in recent years that sympathetic White people who want to have "the talk" with Black friends can come across as seeking absolution for themselves rather than making a deeper commitment to taking actions to make things better. I told him he had a point. It's tempting at times for us to say, "What took you so long?" Certainly, we can do a better job teaching Black history and educating ourselves about the continuing biases that hold Black people back.

But Rick has done a lot more here than discover the obvious. His digging into some issues—redlining, environmental racism, White privilege, reparations—is painful to read about at times but also enlightening. And he has found plenty that was new to me. As a proud alumnus of Howard University, for instance, I found his chapter "Reconstruction"—about our founder, Oliver Otis Howard, the first head of the Freedmen's Bureau after the Civil War—to be fascinating. Ever the newsman, Rick has found fresh material on characters ranging from Lyndon Johnson, to my old colleague Hosea Williams, to Joel Chandler Harris and Uncle Remus.

As a student of the "Atlanta Way," the longtime coalition of White business executives and Black political leaders that helped make Atlanta the capital of the New South—and brought us the Olympics—Rick appreciates the need for people of diverse backgrounds and interests to talk with one another, even if it's difficult, because that is the only way out of no way.

AUTHOR'S NOTE

The scene was a dinner party in Buckhead, the finger bowl district of Atlanta, one night in the 1980s. Our hostess was Jeanne Ferst, a prominent liberal Republican, and the guest of honor was a freshly appointed distinguished professor of something or other at Emory University. What, he asked at one point, did we consider the greatest issue confronting Atlanta? I caught the eye of Michael Lomax, one of my tablemates, an elegant Black man who served as chairman of the Fulton County Commission. "Well," I said, "there's race." Lomax had a twinkle in his eye. "Yes," he added, "and then there's race." I finished: "And of course, race." We chuckled, pleased with our cleverness. Looking back, I'd say we were right on the money.

I came to Atlanta in 1972, a couple of years out of the University of North Carolina, where I studied journalism and admired the steadying hand of Ralph McGill at the *Atlanta Constitution* during the civil rights movement. After weeks of pestering the editors, I got myself hired as a cub reporter in December 1972, right on the cusp of interesting change. Jimmy Carter was governor, Lester Maddox was lieutenant governor, Sam Massell was mayor of Atlanta, and Maynard Jackson was vice mayor. In the space of the next three years, Carter would be president, Jackson would defeat Massell to become the city's first Black mayor, and

Maddox would be rejected by Georgia's voters, once and for all. I began to cover race, a subject that would intrigue and often confound me for the next half century.

Not only was race wickedly complicated, I found, it was also a moving target. Once, doing research in a college library, I came across a copy of *Ebony* magazine from February 1953. The cover showed a formal photograph of Eleanor Roosevelt under a headline that announced, "Some of My Best Friends Are Negroes." I disrupted the decorum of the reading room as I let out a whoop of laughter. What was taken as an earnest expression of liberal goodwill a year before *Brown v. Board of Education* would, in the relative blink of an eye, become a clumpy cliché no White person would dare utter. What struck me then, and still does, is how difficult the races have found it to understand one another and empathize.

I look back at my career as a journey, by a latter-day de Tocqueville, or perhaps Gulliver, traversing the South in search of understanding how two races could share a history at once so intimate and so wicked that love and hate reside side by side, intertwined. As a reporter, columnist, television commentator, and author, I had a front-row seat to the drama, and I mean to review it in this book, for my own benefit and, I hope, for yours.

I have organized this book into three arcs. The first six essays describe events I covered for the newspaper, giving me insights into race and how the subject was evolving before my eyes in ways both subtle and dramatic. Next, starting with "Presidents," I have five essays that deal in a wide variety of ways with US presidents and issues of race. And then, beginning with "Colorblind," I have written about my later efforts, as an author and observer, to study race more closely and dig deeper beneath the surface, even as race relations in America were shifting rapidly in real time. I hope these later essays convey a sincere—and coherent—effort to resolve some of the questions that continue to devil us.

I was well into retirement, in October 2015, when I attended a charette—that's a fancy term for a daylong gabfest—at the Atlanta History Center, held to solicit ideas for updating an exhibit on the city's history. As we gathered in the members room around a large, four-sided table, I was struck by the diversity of the scholars. I knew some of the other older White men, but there were lots of new faces as well—young, female, African American, Latina—who would not have been invited just a generation before.

I found a seat next to a well-dressed young woman, and the session began, as these things often do, by our going around the table introducing ourselves. I explained that I was an old newspaperman who had discovered after twenty years in journalism that I hated news and took to writing books instead. My seatmate turned out to be Gabriela Gonzalez-Lamberson, an aristocratic Mexican émigré with an impressive résumé in corporate public relations, diplomacy, and philanthropy.

Once the formal session began, we discussed Atlanta's history in predictable terms of Black and White, but eventually the conversation turned to the city's growing Hispanic community, and it was then that Gabriela spoke up. To illustrate how closely the cultures of Mexico and the United States are interwoven, she told the story of Joel Poinsett, a South Carolinian who served as the first US minister to Mexico after it achieved independence in the 1820s. Poinsett was an amateur botanist, and he was beguiled by the red flower that Mexicans used in their celebration of Christmas. He sent samples back home, and in short order the US adopted the flower as a seasonal decoration of its own—and named it *poinsettia* in his honor. A charming story, but it was interrupted by a very loud voice from the other side of the table, demanding: "You mean Poinsett . . . *the slave owner*???" The voice belonged to an African American woman, a scholar from Duke University, and I've never forgotten it. So rude. So abrupt. So final. So much for Poinsett! He was a slave owner, and that defined him in his entirety, stripping him of any worth whatsoever. Gabriela fell silent, looking chagrined.

I will confess that I said nothing at the time because I had barely heard of Poinsett and knew almost nothing about him. Perhaps that was true of others as well, because we quickly dropped the subject. But later that night, I looked him up—well, I googled him—and discovered an intriguing figure. Poinsett was widely traveled, erudite, a state legislator, a congressman, a diplomat, a conniver in South American politics (he tried to buy Texas, unsuccessfully, several years before the US took it), and more to the point, he was an ardent Unionist who stood up to John C. Calhoun during the nullification crisis of the 1830s. He owned slaves—and I understand why that's the end of the discussion for many—but he also advocated the gradual abolition of slavery. He opposed secession. He served with a group of gentlemen scholars who were the precursors of the Smithsonian Society. If one wanted to dismiss Poinsett with a thumbs-down, it would be for his role as President Martin Van Buren's secretary of war, when he oversaw the western removal of vast numbers of Native Americans on the Trail of Tears. The point, of course, is that Joel Poinsett was a good deal more complicated and consequential a character than can be conveyed simply in the phrase "slave owner."

During the charette, I decided I wanted to meet the scholar with the booming voice. At the next break, I went over and introduced myself, and she turned out to be perfectly cordial and friendly. We chatted briefly about this and that, and later we corresponded via email, trying to sort through some of the persistent, unresolved questions of race in America. Obviously, I do not agree with the wholesale dismissal of every figure in our nation's history who owned slaves for the simple reason that slavery was legal and a fact of life from 1619 until Emancipation, and White men who owned slaves were prominent among our Founding Fathers. But neither, I have learned, can we possibly come to terms with our past or present if we ignore the raw reality of slavery and its legacy.

My purpose in this book is to dial down the loud voices. I am fully aware that for much of our history, Black men and women have had to shout to be heard—have had to march, protest, suffer, and too often die to be heard. African American readers of this book will find the subject matter painful, often infuriating, and they may question the tone of detachment I've tried to maintain. Partly it's a matter of my training as a reporter, an instinct to be an observer and not a participant. There is a cynical old adage that the job of the journalist is to sit in the hills above the field of battle, and when the fighting is over, go down and shoot the wounded. It's funny when applied to covering ordinary politics, not funny at all when it comes to covering race. I do not mean to shoot the wounded.

As an author, I have always tried to trust the reader. If I set out the facts properly, you get to draw your own conclusions, without me perched on your shoulder telling you what to think and how to feel. As a rule, if something I write makes you angry, it's because I hoped it would but left it up to you. But there's more to it than that. The injustices inflicted on Black Americans have not been inflicted on me. I cannot, as President Clinton famously liked to say, "feel your pain." I can try to empathize, but I am unable to know what it feels like to experience racism. Indeed, I know that in the hearts and minds of many African Americans, I am part of the problem simply by being White and enjoying the White privilege that entails. "You learned *yesterday* what White privilege means?" Damon Young wrote in a scathing op-ed in the *New York Times*. "Great! Welcome to 1962."

Another Black writer, Aisha Harris, described attending a screening of the movie *12 Years a Slave*. "As the mostly White audience trickled out at the end," she wrote, "I heard a man expressing relief to his companion: 'I couldn't last 12 minutes of all that, never mind 12 *years!*'" She called it a "gross comment." I think I know what the man meant—that he found the cruelties of slavery so unspeakable he could not imagine enduring them. But what Harris heard was a White man failing to realize that he would indeed have lasted twelve years because he would have had absolutely no choice to do otherwise.

There are books by White authors—*America's Original Sin*, by Jim Wallis, is one of them—that convey a fully "woke" sensibility, a renunciation of "whiteness," and a redeemer's vow to make things right. This is not one of those books. As a good friend chided me, gently I hope, "Rick, I'm not sure your eyes are as open as you think they are." I am telling my own flawed story here, and it's about my efforts to listen and learn. Readers will have to judge whether I have succeeded.

"BUNCH"

Mama King's funeral.

On July 3, 1974, a torch-hot summer Wednesday in Atlanta, the funeral for Mrs. King was held at her family's historic church, Ebenezer Baptist. As a reporter for the morning newspaper, the *Atlanta Constitution*, I was assigned to cover the ceremony, and I took my place in the front row of the balcony with a handful of other journalists.

The mother of Dr. Martin Luther King Jr. had been playing the church organ during Sunday services four days earlier when a lunatic gunman sprang forward and shot her in the face, killing her, an act that added another layer of unimaginable sorrow onto a family that had suffered on an epic scale. Daddy King already had lost both of his sons, Martin to an assassin and A. D. to drowning, and now his beloved wife, Alberta, had been taken too. The Kings were called "Mama" and "Daddy" by all Atlantans, Black and White alike, because they had come to seem like the city's first family. Journalists like to say we write the first draft of history, and I felt a sharp sense of the weight of the moment and my duty to record it properly.

I'm still not sure how he managed to gather himself, but Daddy King gave one of the eulogies. With three family members steadying him, he told the congregants, "I knew I was going to be strong today. I'm not going to quit. I'm not going to let nothing stop me." And then, in a moment I will never forget, tears began to stream down his face, he raised his eyes to the heavens, and with a wavering voice, he said . . . well, that is the point of my story. I had no idea. I could not understand what he said.

I felt a stab of panic, my pen frozen over my reporter's notebook. I was seated next to Kathryn Johnson, the Associated Press's legendary civil rights reporter, who knew the King family intimately, and I asked her what had just happened. She explained to me that he had said, "I'll be joinin' you soon, Bunch." I hadn't known that his pet name for Mrs. King was "Honeybunch," nor that he was promising to see her in heaven. I will always be grateful to Kathryn for bailing me out. It is a plain truth that journalism is a learning process, and it begins, not ends, when one graduates from J-school. For a White man learning to cover race in the South, I found it was often a steep curve.

I chuckle ruefully sometimes when I encounter the phrase "White privilege." It is meant to convey the myriad advantages that accrue to those born White in America—which is certainly true—but I was born with considerable privilege over other White people as well. My family was wealthy and well-connected. I grew up in Bronxville, New York, a village of about six thousand comfortable souls perched in large houses on small, hilly lots in Westchester County, just north of New York City. There was not a single Black family living in my hometown. I attended Phillips

Academy, in Andover, Massachusetts, with a handful of Black classmates I barely knew. At the University of North Carolina, in the late 1960s, I came to embrace the liberal politics of the era, including civil rights, but I did so largely in the abstract because the student body was still overwhelmingly White. We marched in protest of the treatment of Black cafeteria workers on campus, but I never met any of them.

There is a cliché about the regional difference in White peoples' attitudes toward Black people: In the North, it goes, White people tend to like Black people as a group but not so much individually, while the reverse is true in the South, where Whites disdain Black people collectively but have warm relationships with individuals. Like most clichés, it contains a large kernel of truth. De facto segregation in the North often kept Whites so far removed from Black people that they knew few if any of them and were stiff and uncomfortable in their rare encounters. In the South, on the other hand, segregation was de jure—White supremacy encoded as the law of the land—but Black and White people lived near one another, interacted frequently, and had close, even loving relationships. As a White man from the North, I have spent a half century trying to understand how Black and White people in the South manage these relationships when they are freighted with such inequality. In the early going, though, I just tried to understand what Black people were saying. There was no foreign language course at Chapel Hill to train my Yankee ear, and so I had to learn on the job.

Of course, there was no shortage of erudite Black people in Atlanta when I began work at the *Constitution* in 1972. Maynard Jackson was elected the city's first Black mayor in 1973, and he had a vocabulary that he wielded like a lightsaber. A preacher's son

with a law degree, Jackson was equally adept at sermons and sum-
mations, delivering both in a booming baritone. I vividly recall
an early press conference when he was asked a sticky question
and responded, "I find such assertions to be specious, illogical,
vapid, inane—and juh-joooon." I understood each word clearly,
although the last one, *jejune*, sent me to the dictionary. Jackson
once ended an interview with me by saying, "In the words of
Tea and Sympathy, Rick, when you think of me tonight—*and you
will*—be kind." Another time I bumped into him at the Atlanta
Civic Center during the intermission of a Richard Pryor concert
and asked what he thought. "Scatological," he answered, enunci-
ating each syllable, "but a comic genius!"

My problem was understanding poorer Blacks, especially in
the rural areas of Georgia. I was no longer a cub reporter when
I covered the case of the Dawson Five, in 1977, but I had not
made much progress with translation. Largely forgotten today,
the Dawson Five were an earlier, South Georgia version of the
Central Park Five. Five young Black men had been charged with
the murder of a White customer during a holdup in a country
store in a remote corner of Terrell County. Their defense lawyer,
Millard Farmer, was a prominent opponent of the death penalty
from Atlanta, and his strategy was simple. He planned to put the
city of Dawson on trial for racism. My involvement began when
Farmer, who was White, drove me out into the countryside of
Terrell County to visit the family of two of the defendants, who
were brothers. Their mother granted me an interview, and when it
was over and Farmer and I were walking back to his car, he looked
into my reporter's notebook and began laughing. I hadn't written
down a single word because I could not understand a thing the
woman said. Farmer assured me that she had professed her sons'

innocence, but otherwise had not provided any material information about the case.

As it happened, though, the point of our visit was not so much her words as the abject poverty the family lived in. Their house was a crude shack, and I can still see the flattened, rusted snuff tins that dotted the wooden floor, covering its many holes. Of course, being poor did not absolve the defendants of murder, but Farmer meant for our trip to set the stage for what was to come. In a pretrial hearing a few days later, he put a former Dawson policeman on the stand who testified that a fellow officer had questioned one of the defendants, seventeen-year-old James Jackson Jr., by cocking his pistol, placing it between the boy's eyes, and saying, "Okay, nigger, where's the gun at?"

The hearing was a feast of horrors. The former policeman also testified that two officers on the Dawson force regularly amused themselves by feeding arsenic-laced dog food to Black people's pets, an accusation that drew gasps in the courtroom. At times it seemed the city meant to convict itself. Farmer put the mayor of Dawson, James G. Raines Jr., on the stand and asked about the city's Whites-only swimming pool. The city had built the pool with bonds underwritten by taxpayers of both races but then sold it for a nominal fee to a private club that allowed only White people to use it. Raines, a refined man with a Harvard law degree, seemed pained to admit the inequity, and when Farmer asked if he would authorize the arrest of Black children who tried to use the pool, he said he would not. "Well," Farmer responded, "I guess we'll try to have a swimming party!" Late that evening, the pool was drained and closed indefinitely behind barbed wire.

It was not my ear for language that failed me back then so much as myopia, as I missed the portent of some of the changes

taking place before my eyes. With the benefit of hindsight, I realize that I was witnessing the eclipse of the overt, bare-knuckled
racism that erupted throughout the South after the Supreme
Court's *Brown v. Board of Education* decision in 1954, which
undid the "separate but equal" doctrine that had been the law
of the land, and the foundation of Jim Crow, for more than half
a century. The tools of massive resistance—the fire hoses and
German shepherds, the Klan bonfires, the church bombings, the
assassinations—had by now brought revulsion to the nation. The
passage of the Civil Rights Act of 1964 and the Voting Rights
Act of 1965 were, like glaciers, slowly but inexorably scraping
away many of the barriers that had kept Black people from full
citizenship in their native land.

What I saw and heard in court in 1977 appalled me, of course,
as it was meant to do. But I should have recognized that these
were the last throes of a culture in retreat. For one thing, I was in
absolutely no physical danger whatsoever. An earlier generation
of journalists had faced genuine menace covering the civil rights
movement, including those who traveled to "Terrible Terrell," as
the county was nicknamed, in 1962, after two Black churches
were burned to ash and cinder because they had hosted rallies in
support of Black voter registration. With help from the Kennedy
administration, the churches were rebuilt, and my colleague Bill
Shipp shared a vivid memory of covering a voter registration drive
at one of them when the sheriff of Terrell County, the formi-
dable Zeke T. Mathews, entered the church, marched up to the
reporters in the front pew, and demanded, "Who are you?" As
Shipp recalled, Claude Sitton of the *New York Times*, a famously
fearless man, stood up chin to chin with Mathews and answered,
"I'm an American, sheriff, how about you?" Shipp said he and

Sitton counted themselves lucky to emerge with only slashed tires to show for the confrontation.

A decade and a half later, those forces were in retreat. Seeking to defuse the Dawson Five situation, the prosecutor in Terrell County's judicial circuit announced that he would not seek the death penalty for the defendants. The judge, Walter I. Geer, permitted Farmer broad leeway in eliciting testimony and evidence of police misconduct, and eventually the state dropped all charges against the young men. I now believe that quiet forces were at work to prevent a miscarriage of justice because Dawson sat just twenty-one miles from Plains, Georgia, the home of President Jimmy Carter, who had entered the White House earlier that year as a "New South" figure who would not have appreciated a travesty of justice in his backyard.

I have one final small, sad, funny memory of the case. During an interview, the police chief was trying to persuade me that Dawson had turned a new leaf. Mayor Raines, he noted, had a law degree from Harvard. "And he's a homosexual," the chief added, as if to certify that a fresh day of urbanity had dawned in his town. Most of the White people I encountered in Dawson were not defiant. They were defensive.

In time, I got better acquainted with Black folks, including Daddy King. For one thing, I learned that friends and family did not call him Daddy but rather just Dad. One day I encountered him in the office of the Fulton County tax commissioner, who liked to do small favors for journalists and prominent citizens. We chatted a bit while the commissioner sent a minion to renew our car registrations. Some years later, I was riding an elevator at the state capitol when King got on, and we exchanged greetings. At the next floor, the doors opened and in stepped J. B. Stoner, one of the most notorious, retrograde segregationists in the state of Georgia, a perennial candidate for high office who ran on a platform of White supremacy and took out newspaper ads disparaging Black people in the crudest terms. King eyed him evenly for a moment. Then he said, "Mr. Stoner, you are a cruel man."

I understood him perfectly.

SEGREGATIONISTS

I met George Wallace exactly once. In November 1979, I drove from Atlanta to Alabama to cover a press conference held by Richard Arrington Jr., who had just been elected Birmingham's first Black mayor. While there, I made a courtesy call on Wallace, who was receiving visiting journalists in a small office. I have one vivid memory of the encounter: Wallace insisted that I feel his upper arm. After years confined to a wheelchair, he had developed tremendous upper-body strength, and his muscles were rock-hard. I felt awkward, as if I had encountered an interactive exhibit in a museum, and withdrew after a few niceties. It did not occur to me to attempt a formal interview because I didn't think there was anything newsworthy to discuss. It turned out I was wrong.

Wallace had completed his third term as governor earlier in the year, and though he told the state legislature, "I suppose my career is over," he had quietly begun planning to run one more time. Around the time of our meeting, Wallace made a private, unannounced visit to the Dexter Avenue Baptist Church in Montgomery, Dr. King's old pulpit, where he renounced his past actions as a segregationist and asked for forgiveness. "I have learned what suffering means," he told the congregation. "In a way that was impossible before [the shooting], I think I can understand something of the pain Black people have come to endure. I know I contributed to that pain, and I can only ask your forgiveness."

The sincerity of Wallace's expression of regret remains a matter of disagreement to this day, of course, but the fact is many of his Black listeners believed him, and their support at the ballot box proved to be the decisive factor when he won his fourth and final term in the fall of 1982. "We're all family down here," Johnny Ford, the mayor of Tuskegee, explained. "That's what the North doesn't understand. We're all family." What Wallace did fascinates me because it occurred around the same time I was writing profiles of two retired "seg" (short for segregationist, in the parlance of the day) politicians in Georgia—former Governor Marvin Griffin and former House Speaker Roy V. Harris—and I had trouble reconciling the hateful things they had said and done in the past with the warm and likable personalities they displayed when I spent time with them. It bothered me then and still does.

In the late autumn of 1977, not long after my experience covering the Dawson Five, I drove from Atlanta down to Bainbridge, Georgia, a small city in the southwest corner of the state, to interview Griffin. "You can't spend five minutes with Marvin," a friend warned me, "without liking him." I arrived at the offices of his family's weekly newspaper, the *Post-Searchlight*, and was shown to the back of the shop, where Griffin sat at a desk in front of a large painting that depicted an astonished-looking Grant surrendering to Lee at Appomattox. Naturally I did a double take. "Well,"

Griffin said wistfully, his blue eyes dancing, "it could have been." I had to laugh.

Griffin presented me with a serious challenge, one I still have not resolved. Serving as governor from 1955 to 1959, he had been as unrelenting a segregationist as could be found anywhere in the South, a stalwart of massive resistance in the same league with Wallace and Ross Barnett. "I take my stand with the white people," he announced when he began his campaign, and he kept the promise. In 1957, he traveled to Little Rock, Arkansas, and helped incite the violence that erupted over the desegregation of Central High School.

But it turned out that Griffin was also warm, funny, direct, and immensely likable. At the end of my visit, he bade me farewell with an invitation to return. "We'll cook a steak," he said, "bend an elbow, strike a blow for liberty, and talk about everybody!" How could I reconcile his magnetism with the hateful actions he had taken in the past? Naively, I soft-pedaled his racism in the profile I wrote for the *Constitution*, suggesting that he was motivated more by political expediency than racial animus. "There was a sense," I wrote, "that Griffin used 'seg' propaganda simply because that was the order of the day in Georgia politics." Well, no. He was charming *and* a racist—both things in a single package. When I interviewed him, he made it clear that he did not wish to talk about race. "They'll just say I was a racist," he had told an interviewer a few years earlier, "and we've already been through all that." I let him off the hook.

I had a similar experience two years later, in 1979, when I wrote a profile of Roy Harris, another legendary segregationist. "Mr. Roy," as he was known, was eighty-three at the time, retired from politics after a career as a state legislator, longtime regent of the University System of Georgia, and kingmaker in gubernatorial elections over the decades. He had a courtly air, a warm smile, and a virtual case of amnesia about his record, which included serving as Wallace's campaign manager in Georgia in 1968. "There's really only going to be one issue," he said at the time, "and you spell it n-i-g-g-e-r." A decade later, when I encountered him, he blithely assured me, "I don't think I've ever lost a black friend around Augusta." Had I been impertinent, I might have asked if he'd ever *had* a Black friend in Augusta.

Having learned my lesson two years earlier with Griffin, I did not make the mistake of excusing Harris's racism as a mere political expedient. I pointed out one of his lowest moments, when he opposed the appointment of former secretary of state Dean Rusk as a professor of international law at the University of Georgia, in large part because Rusk's daughter had married a Black man. I conceded that at one time, most successful White politicians in Georgia had been segregationists, but added, "It was only when the others began to change, like the evolution from darkness to light in an Escher print, that Harris stood out as a radical racist." I did let Harris have his say. "You haven't seen me agitating one way or the other" in recent years, he told me, and I duly included his disclaimer in my article. I treated him gently enough that the editors wrote a headline saying, "Mr. Roy: Still Scrappy—There's a Lot More to Him Than Racist Image."

So what might I have done differently? I think I should have pressed both men on their feelings about race and whether they had evolved. Neither one volunteered the sort of apology that Wallace gave the congregants at the Dexter Avenue church, but I've been struck over the years by the sincere regret expressed by some politicians who came to see the light, as Wallace apparently did. Griffin, in particular, strikes me as a victim of his own sense of humor. He once was asked about J. B. Stoner, the violent racist. "He reminds me," Griffin said, "of the story about the drunk on the *Titanic* who raced out on the deck and said, 'I ordered ice, but this is ridiculous!'" It is impossible for me to imagine any Black person finding that joke amusing. I suppose Griffin felt that parsing the exact degree of his racism was a futile exercise, but some measure of confession might have been good for his soul.

Of course, one very real possibility is that Griffin and Harris did not harbor any regrets at all. But my best guess is that both men would have insisted that they merely believed the races should remain separate in the best interests of both, and that they bore no ill will toward Black people. In an interview with the *New York Times* in January 1979, Wallace tested such an argument, saying he was motivated by states' rights and not racial prejudice. "I was not an enemy of blacks in those days," he said, hearkening back to the 1960s. "I was the enemy of the federal government, big government. It's very unfortunate that it involved race when we raised those issues." He added, "I was never saying anything that reflected on black people, and I'm sorry it was taken that way."

Just months later, recognizing how hollow those sentiments rang, he issued his full-throated apology at the Dexter Avenue church. He also met with civil rights leader John Lewis, who said, "I could tell that he was a changed man. He was engaged in a campaign to seek forgiveness from the same African Americans he had oppressed. He acknowledged his bigotry and assumed responsibility for the harm he had caused. He wanted to be forgiven."

As it happened, both Griffin and Harris went to their graves a few years after I interviewed them, neither having renounced his racism. Griffin, a smoker, died of lung cancer in 1982 at age seventy-four. It fell to a bitter rival, former Governor Carl Sanders, to volunteer a very generous benediction. "On a personal level," he said of Griffin, "he never mistreated anyone. I think he did use it [segregation] to a political advantage, but, ultimately, he believed everyone was equal both in the sight of God and under the law." I would like to believe those words were true—but I'm afraid I don't.

Harris died in 1985, never having recanted. "I'm a segregationist, yeah," he once insisted. "I make no bones about that." Yet there was a footnote. In 1981, he gave his support to a Black man, Ed McIntyre, who was elected the first Black mayor of Augusta—and McIntyre named him city attorney in return. So Harris had made his peace on at least one matter of race.

In researching this essay, I came across a remarkable article from the *New York Times* Sunday magazine, one that so far as I know had been lost to history. The editors traveled to Atlanta in 1969 and asked Harris and Julian Bond, then a state legislator, to meet at the Commerce Club for a discussion about race. Both men were on their best behavior and conversed cordially and earnestly. "I do think," Harris said at one point, "as a general rule, you ought to have separate schools and separate churches." Afterward, Bond wrote an assessment of Harris: "But what a contradiction. There is no open meanness in him, no vitriol like that in those who read his sheet [the *Augusta Courier*], none of the open, quick hatred that causes children at prayer to face bombs and makes big, brave men use baseball bats to keep children from their ABC's." For his part, Harris was polite. "I've always said the race problem can't be solved without a mutual agreement between the races, and you can't ever get together without more dialogues like the one Bond and I had."

Politicians tend to be attractive people, and I certainly found Griffin and Harris to be charming. No surprise there. I believe that if I had questioned them more forcefully, they likely would have tried the first argument Wallace made, that their cause was racial separatism and not bigotry. It's anyone's guess if they would have recognized the emptiness of that claim and moved a few steps down the path of genuine apology and atonement, but I owed them—and our readers, and myself—the chance to try.

ATLANTA CHILD MURDERS

The Atlanta Child Murders were, by definition, a crime story. But looking back forty years later, it seems to me they more closely resembled a horror movie or a novel of science fiction. Black children were mysteriously disappearing and dying, as if snatched by aliens for reasons of unfathomable evil, and no explanation seemed plausible, not even when a suspect was caught, tried, and convicted. Our criminal justice system works pretty well with most types of crimes, but it is ill-suited to handle matters of race.

At the outset, on August 28, 1979, when the first two bodies were discovered in a vacant, wooded lot on Niskey Lake Road, things unfolded about as one might expect—slowly. No identifications were made because the bodies were badly decomposed, and police could not even tell at first if they were male or female. One can certainly wonder, as I do, if a greater sense of urgency might have arisen had the bodies been found in a better neighborhood, or if some prominent citizen's child had been reported missing. But the corpses were abandoned in a trash-strewn lot. At that point, I believe, the key factor was poverty, not race.

Several months later, when the body count had risen to half a dozen, all of them Black children, the situation reached critical mass. Camille Bell, the mother of one of the victims, nine-year-old Yusuf Bell, formed the Committee to Stop Children's Murders and began pressing the police to investigate. Hesitant at first to confirm that a serial killer might be on the loose, the Atlanta police finally relented and formed a task force in July 1980. By then the cases had acquired a nickname, the "Missing and Murdered," as the media reported the sensational news that a murderer appeared to be targeting the city's Black children.

Understandably, Atlanta's Black community was seized by fear. I recall encountering a young Black mother in an office at city hall around that time, and the dread she exuded over the safety of her children was palpable. Given the history of race in America, it is hardly surprising that Black and White people responded differently as the reports of missing children and the discovery of bodies mounted. Many Black people suspected a race war might be underway, with the Ku Klux Klan snatching Black boys off the streets. Many Whites reasoned that White men cruising Black neighborhoods trying to pick up Black children would stand out and might be in some danger themselves. It was human nature to hope the culprit was not of one's own race.

A pivotal moment occurred on the morning of Monday, October 13, 1980, when a boiler exploded in a day care center at the Bowen Homes housing project, killing four toddlers and a teacher, leaving a scene that looked like a war zone. Investigators suspected an accident, not a bomb, but at first many of the residents believed they had been attacked, a fear fueled when anonymous, threatening phone calls were received later in the morning at several schools, day care centers, and housing projects around the city, prompting closures. When Mayor Maynard Jackson arrived at Bowen Homes and urged calm, he was jeered.

That evening, a thousand residents of Bowen Homes gathered at Greater Fair Hill Baptist Church in a mood of extreme agitation. Efforts by Police Chief George Napper and Public Safety Commissioner Lee Brown to reassure the crowd that the explosion was an accident provoked anger that bordered on chaos. Violence seemed possible. The hero of the moment turned out to be Hosea Williams, the legendary civil rights leader who served as a lieutenant to Martin Luther King Jr. in the Southern Christian Leadership Conference, and a wily man of greater depths than many realized. On the spot, Williams organized a march on city hall—a march that took two hours, covered five long miles, and left a mob sapped of energy standing isolated and harmless on the deserted streets of downtown Atlanta in the dead of night.

Within a day, investigators established that the blast was indeed an accident. The boiler, poorly maintained and equipped with a disabled safety device, had blown up after it was turned on for the first time of the fall season on a chilly morning. The panic over the explosion ended, but Chet Fuller, a well-respected Black reporter with the *Atlanta Journal*, wrote a news analysis later that week with a chilly, cautionary headline, "Racial Peace Can't Be Taken for Granted."

The feeling grew among some in the Black community that more would have been done if the victims had been White. In November, a month after the Bowen Homes incident, Mayor Jackson lashed out at the director of the FBI, William Webster, for failing to assign more agents to the case. "Lindbergh was one child," Jackson said, referring to the sensational abduction of Charles Lindbergh's son in the 1930s, "and we're talking about 15 here!"

It is worth pointing out that Jackson was Black, as were his commissioner of public safety and police chief, and there was certainly no dereliction of duty on their parts. Indeed, it seemed to me that the cases drew abundant attention and response, almost to the point of becoming a circus. Contributions flowed in, psychics arrived, special investigators volunteered their time. The FBI assigned more agents. At one point, Jackson posed in front of an enormous pile of $100,000 in cash being offered as reward money. The Guardian Angels flew in from New York, while a homegrown vigilante group, the "Bat Patrol," fanned out in Techwood Homes. Small armies of volunteers deployed every weekend to search lots and woods for the missing. People wore "We Care" buttons. Frank Sinatra and Sammy Davis Jr. gave a concert at the civic center to raise money and awareness. President Ronald Reagan, newly inaugurated in January 1981, sent nearly $1 million in federal funds for youth programs and a twenty-four-hour hotline. Robert De Niro wore a green ribbon in recognition of the victims when he won the Academy Award that spring for *Raging Bull*.

The investigation ground on. The authorities devoted enormous manpower and time to the cases, as reflected in the overtime pay earned by Atlanta police. The task force employed sophisticated profiling techniques devised by the FBI to focus their search for the killer. The pattern of the murders evolved to older, adult victims, most likely because Atlanta's Black children had been counseled endlessly by parents, teachers, psychologists, and security experts to be vigilant, thus shrinking the target population. As the count rose to twenty-eight, several of the later victims were discovered in the Chattahoochee River, arguably an easier, safer venue than city streets for disposing of bodies. The police began staking out the bridges over the Chattahoochee, and in the wee hours of the morning of May 22, 1981, they got the break they had been seeking. A recruit conducting surveillance under the James Jackson Parkway bridge was startled by a loud splash. He radioed for backup, and moments later police pulled over a white station wagon driven by a light-skinned Black man named Wayne Williams.

The task force was confident from the outset that Williams, a twenty-three-year-old talent agent, was their man. But proving it would be a daunting challenge. The source of the splash could not be discovered that morning in the dark. Williams was questioned and released. Two days later, the body of Nathaniel Cater was found downstream on the banks of the river, and the investigation of Williams went into overdrive. Pudgy, standing just five foot seven, he did not seem physically menacing, but his work as a budding record producer brought him into frequent contact with aspiring young singers and suggested how he might have gained the confidence of the victims.

It is not my purpose to put Williams back on trial. But one important point needs to be made. An idea has persisted for decades that Williams was railroaded by overeager police and prosecutors desperate to solve the child murders in order to protect Atlanta's reputation or even to avert a race war. A corollary theory was that Atlanta's White business leaders, worried about Atlanta's image, pressured a quiescent Mayor Jackson into making Williams a scapegoat. This is nonsense. Investigators of every stripe—Black, White, local, state, and federal—were convinced that Williams committed the murders and pushed for his arrest and indictment. One of the strongest voices for prosecution belonged to John Glover, the agent-in-charge of Atlanta's FBI office, a Black man. It was the prosecutor, Fulton County District Attorney Lewis Slaton, a White man, who held things up, and he did so for a reason familiar to anyone who has ever read a crime novel: he wanted more time, more evidence, a tighter case, and better odds of gaining a conviction.

I knew Slaton well. We met in January 1973, when I was assigned to cover the Fulton County courthouse. During our first interview in his office, Slaton busied himself with a hairpin, picking open the lock of the center drawer of his desk, a trick meant to show me I was dealing with a wily character, as indeed I was.

In the weeks after becoming the prime suspect, Williams engaged in a game of cat and mouse with the authorities, mocking their efforts to build a case against him. He held press conferences, passed out his résumé to reporters, led police on high-speed car chases around town, including one that went past Mayor Jackson's house, and generally thumbed his nose at his pursuers. Their push to arrest and prosecute him flowed more from embarrassment and anger at his antics than any sort of racial politics. But Slaton stood in the way.

Mayor Jackson, bolstered by a decision from his public safety commissioner that the arrest and indictment of Williams were warranted and overdue, arranged a meeting at the White House with President Reagan on Wednesday, June 17, 1981, ostensibly to brief him on the case but mostly to stage a photo opportunity intended to show the two men—a Black Democrat and White Republican—united in wanting to see the case brought to trial.

The next day, acting US Attorney Dorothy Kirkley and FBI Agent Glover flew from Atlanta to Washington, DC, armed with a thick briefing book and laid out their case against Williams for members of the Justice Department's Criminal Division. That afternoon, Deputy Attorney General Edward Schmults called the governor of Georgia, George Busbee, and arranged a meeting of principals for the next morning at the governor's mansion, meant to prod Slaton into action. It was a remarkable session, well worth recounting, described to me in detail at the time by several of the participants. As Slaton sat scowling, Kirkley argued adamantly in favor of proceeding with the criminal case. Slaton shot back that the FBI had botched the investigation by failing to arrest Williams and search his car on the morning of the splash. And he openly worried that after the FBI handed over the case, they would wash their hands of it and leave him holding the bag. The meeting ended in stalemate, but the FBI's Glover made a strong point that Williams was a flight risk. Two days later, when Williams and his father were found to be making inquiries about hiring a private pilot, Slaton relented and ordered the arrest.

I cannot recall anyone objecting. There were skeptics, certainly, starting with Camille Bell, who strongly doubted that Williams had killed all twenty-nine victims on the list. But the Black community generally seemed to be relieved. Members of the task force also doubted that Williams had committed all of the murders, but it seemed a poor idea to provoke controversy by crossing any victims off the list, especially since doing so might cast suspicion of neglect or domestic violence onto the families of those removed.

As Slaton feared, the case proved problematic. His office elected to indict Williams for the murder of only two of the victims: Cater, twenty-seven, and Jimmy Ray Payne, twenty-one, both adults. From a trial standpoint, it made sense to go for verdicts in the two strongest cases, but that meant the book on the child murders would be closed without a single conviction for the murder of a child—a sharp, disturbing irony. The prosecution is remembered for relying heavily on evidence that matched carpet fibers taken from Williams's station wagon with fibers found on Cater, Payne, and other victims. Inside the courtroom, the fiber evidence seemed persuasive, but it proved elusive to the larger public. Other evidence was compelling as well, including witnesses who placed Williams with some of the victims. And Williams, who insisted on testifying, famously undid himself with an aggressive performance during cross-examination, at one point telling the prosecutor, "You must be a fool."

In February 1982, after a nine-week trial, a jury of eight Black people and four White people took only eleven hours to return guilty verdicts on both counts. Williams was given two life sentences and sent to prison. The task force declared that Williams was responsible for killing all but two of the victims, the two females, and then disbanded.

There were disquieting signs from the start. Camille Bell greeted the verdict with open derision, proclaiming Williams innocent. The parents of other victims expressed uncertainty. As a headline in the *Atlanta Journal* put it, "Families of Victims Still Yearning for Answers." Jimmy Payne's sister, Evelyn, told the newspaper, "I still don't know if they have the right man." Two days after the trial, defense lawyer Alvin Binder suggested on ABC's *Nightline* that he knew of additional slayings of young Black victims after his client was arrested, an accusation that gained currency when an independent investigator, Chet Dettlinger, wrote a book, *The List*, that insisted dozens of murders continued after Williams was off the streets.

One of the procedural quirks of the trial also raised eyebrows. Judge Clarence Cooper allowed the state to introduce so-called pattern evidence tying Williams to ten of the other victims, even though he was not charged in their deaths. When the issue was raised on appeal, the Georgia Supreme Court upheld the guilty verdict, but one of the justices, George Smith, issued a lengthy, stinging dissent, calling the admission of pattern evidence "highly prejudicial" and casting doubt on the state's entire case.

Nothing did more to undermine faith in the convictions than a five-hour docudrama, *The Atlanta Child Murders*, that aired on CBS in February 1985. The screenwriter, Abby Mann, made his perspective clear by having the narrator, Morgan Freeman, call Wayne Williams "a sacrificial lamb on the altar of Atlanta." I recall watching the show at the time with a sense of disbelief. The central thesis was that Mayor Jackson and other Black leaders were bullied into rigging a case against Williams by a White business community fearful that the child murders were bad for business. Anyone familiar with Maynard Jackson—"Action Jackson," as he styled himself, "large and in charge"—knew well that he took no marching orders from the White executives in Atlanta's boardrooms, or anyone else for that matter. I considered it a form of liberal Hollywood racism to make such a suggestion. One small cruelty of the movie was its caricature of Judge Cooper, the first Black judge to serve on the Fulton County Superior Court, as a servile flunky with a street accent who called the court "de cote." I knew Judge Cooper, who went on to a distinguished career on the federal bench, and he deserved better.

There was more to come. In November 1985, a "dream team" of fresh defense lawyers, headed by Harvard's Alan Dershowitz and Georgia's famed Bobby Lee Cook, filed a new appeal based on their discovery that the Georgia Bureau of Investigation had pursued a tip from an informant that a member of the Ku Klux Klan once threatened one of the victims on the list, Lubie Geter, during a street encounter. The tip did not pan out, but the lawyers argued that the state should have given the information to Williams's original defense team. The appeals courts did not agree, but the very mention of the Klan was predictably explosive. The next year, a pair of articles in *Spin* magazine advanced the theory that the Klan was attempting to foment a race war by abducting and killing a Black youth every month.

Given the sensational developments, it is a wonder that the child murder cases then went dormant for almost two decades. The investigation was reopened in 2005 by Louis Graham, the police chief in DeKalb County, where five of the victims lived, but it unearthed no new information and was closed without fanfare. In 2019, Mayor Keisha Lance Bottoms announced that the authorities would take another look at the cases, using DNA testing and other modern methods—an avenue that had yet to yield any fresh information by the spring of 2023. She noted that she was a nine-year-old when the cases first erupted. "It robbed us of our innocence," she said, "and reminded us evil was real."

It's certainly easy enough to second-guess some of the decisions made forty years ago. Closing the criminal case without trying Williams for the deaths of any of the children may have saved time, money, and the risk of acquittal, but in hindsight it left more than two dozen families without certainty that Williams was the killer. I think the real problem is that the criminal justice system is not equipped to heal the rifts of race. Looking back, I think the Black community was divided along fault lines of class. Black leaders, starting with Mayor Jackson and including his successor,

Andrew Young, had confidence in the investigation and conviction of Wayne Williams. But the families of the victims, poor, ill-served in so many ways for so many years by the powers that be, could not keep faith that justice had been done. Thousands of other Black Atlantans agreed with them.

One reason I believe that Wayne Williams is guilty was that the murders ceased after he was arrested and taken off the streets. I am aware that a number of doubters argue that the murders actually continued. But if they had—if Black children had kept disappearing, their bodies turning up in vacant lots and abandoned buildings and in rivers—then I am confident that the parents and families of those children would have raised holy hell, just as they did when the murders began. They did not. And I trust them.

"Grinning, Shuffling"

In October 1980, two of Martin Luther King Jr.'s top lieutenants committed the apostasy of endorsing Ronald Reagan for president. Ralph David Abernathy and Hosea Williams, neither very close to President Jimmy Carter, threw in their lots with the Republican nominee, to the consternation of some civil rights leaders and the amusement of others.

Abernathy, a proud, ponderous man, treated the matter with utmost seriousness, claiming he had successfully persuaded Reagan to promise the appointment of an African American successor if Supreme Court Justice Thurgood Marshall died or retired. Williams pretty much admitted he hoped to benefit from some payback if Reagan won. One night he regaled a small group of journalists with an account of the visit he and Abernathy made to see Reagan at his home in California on November 5, 1980, the day after the election. Abernathy congratulated the president-elect and reassured him earnestly that he and Williams sought no favors in exchange for their support. Laughing and shaking his head, Williams described how he tried—unsuccessfully—to tug at Abernathy's jacket and signal him not to give up the spoils so easily.

For the most part, Black leaders made light of the defections, because Abernathy and Williams were no longer considered figures of much consequence. I wrote a column I quickly came to regret, passing along a condescending portrait of Abernathy that I gathered from his old colleagues in the movement, calling him irrelevant. He had succeeded King as head of the Southern Christian Leadership Conference, only to see the money and influence dry up as Coretta Scott King raised funds for the King Center, and other leaders—Andrew Young and Jesse Jackson—gained greater prominence. In 1977, Abernathy ran for Young's vacated seat in Congress and finished with only 3,614 votes, less than 5 percent. My headline called him "Poor Ralph." He phoned me the morning it ran and told me I'd been mean-spirited. He was right.

I was kinder to Williams, mostly because I knew him pretty well and liked him. I first encountered him in 1973, my first year at the newspaper, when he was leading workers at Rich's department store in a strike for better pay and conditions. I was dispatched one afternoon to cover the pickets as they gathered at a church before heading to the sidewalk in front of the landmark store in downtown Atlanta. A squat fireplug of a man with a raspy voice, Williams began denouncing the *Constitution*'s coverage of the strike, and as he spoke the strikers began to stare at me and murmur. Williams saw what was happening and nipped it in the bud. "You leave that young man alone," he said, defusing the situation. "He's just doing his job." I appreciated his decorum and decided he was not quite the wild man many believed.

As it happened, Williams did earn a reward from Reagan, and it quickly became the stuff of legend. The White House invited

Williams and his wife, Juanita, to a state dinner honoring the president of Venezuela. The poor people's champion famously donned a tuxedo, arrived via limousine, dined on rack of lamb, and thoroughly enjoyed his evening with the fat cats. He even pocketed an ashtray as a souvenir. "These tuxedos, these limousines, this food," he exulted to a reporter, "God intended for man to have it!"

Williams got away with such things for several reasons. First and foremost, he really was a fighter for the poor. His "Feed the Hungry" program began on Thanksgiving Day 1971, and many years later, long after his death, it remains the largest provider of free holiday meals in Atlanta. His physical courage was a wonder. It was Williams who led the marchers up the Edmund Pettus Bridge in Selma, Alabama, on "Bloody Sunday" in 1965, into the teeth of the deputy sheriffs and state troopers arrayed against them, absorbing a terrible beating along with John Lewis. And there was his sense of humor: he famously turned to Lewis at the top of the bridge and said, "John, do you know how to swim?"

It has been a staple of political commentary for decades that the Black vote is "not monolithic," yet it very often is. The year after Williams and Abernathy broke ranks, a far more dramatic episode of intraracial policing took place, and it shocked me. Maynard Jackson, completing his second four-year term as mayor of Atlanta and barred from running again, set his sights on recruiting Young as his successor. Fresh from service as Carter's United Nations ambassador, Young jumped into the campaign with gusto, figuring he would be a shoo-in. After all, his campaigns for Congress had drawn substantial White support. But this time there would be no coronation.

Jackson's eight years as mayor had left the races divided in Atlanta. There was plenty of blame to go around. The *Atlanta*

Constitution, my employer, had a reputation as a beacon of liberalism thanks to Ralph McGill, the late publisher, whose front-page columns helped pave the way for Atlanta's pragmatic approach to civil rights. But the harsh truth is that we were a White institution, and we greeted Jackson's election with trepidation and suspicion. At first, the friction was gentle. I recall being greeted with guffaws at city hall the morning after Jackson's inaugural. I had written a front-page feature story on the ceremony at the civic center. Struck by the formality of the affair—the Atlanta Symphony played Beethoven's Ninth, and Jackson's aunt Mattiwilda Dobbs, the renowned opera singer, performed an aria and a spiritual for an audience dressed to the nines, many of the women in mink—I described it as being like "a church service."

I was thinking, of course, of my own church—the lily-white, Presbyterian, buttoned-up, Yankee church of my youth—and not of services familiar to Southern Black churchgoers, with amen corners, dancing in the aisles, and enviable exuberance. The mayor's entire staff, it seemed, insisted on wondering aloud what possible "church service" I could have had in mind, and some went so far as to point out that the program had begun and ended exactly on schedule, not on the leisurely "CPT"—Colored People's Time—that typically extended the start and finish of Black church services.

I wish all my coverage of Jackson had been so innocent. I am highly embarrassed to this day over one story I wrote. After moving to Atlanta, the mayor's top administrator, Jule Sugarman, a well-regarded bureaucrat from New York City, had arranged for his daughter to switch high schools from Grady, in whose district they lived, to Northside. It was a minor matter, a slight bending of rules to put the young woman into a school with a better academic record. But the story I wrote made it sound worse than Watergate, and the *Constitution* ran it on the front page under an eight-column headline. I reported that the switch had moved Sugarman's daughter from a predominantly Black school to a mostly White one, an ominous accusation. When the phone rang on my desk first thing the next morning, the caller was a White woman who asked with exasperation if I realized that Grady High School was majority White, just like Northside. I will never forget her scorn when I gulped and admitted that I hadn't bothered to check. I could call it carelessness rather than racial malice, but the truth is, I was part and parcel of an institution that greeted the city's first Black mayor with hostility.

Jackson had been in office slightly more than a year, in March 1975, when our paper ran an infamous series, "City in Crisis," whose premise asserted that Atlanta "was Camelot" in the 1960s but had now lost its way, as "the Jackson administration continues to stumble from one scandal to another." For eight days, we gave voice to the White business community's frustrations dealing with the mayor. Certainly Jackson made his share of missteps, but the series was one-sided, deaf to the voices of the Black community, and highly unsettling to many in the city. Many years later, Jackson and I were on a panel at Emory University, and he caught my attention with the remark that our coverage made him realize that while he had control of his character, he had utterly lost control of his reputation.

The important point, I believe, is that I did not think at the time that my coverage of Jackson had any tinge of racism to it. I liked him personally and considered him smart, attractive, and charismatic. Of course, I was a doctrinaire liberal just a half-decade removed from the college campus where we fancied ourselves free of prejudice and in favor of civil rights. It did not occur to me that I was in the dead center of institutional racism, where our newspaper operated on an underlying assumption that Jackson's agenda—shaped by his race—represented a threat to the "proper" order of things.

I remember how I made my peace with the mayor. One day his top adviser, David Franklin, walked into the press room at city hall, greeted me with a smile, and said, "Rick, why do you write all that shit about Maynard?" We had a candid conversation, in which my instincts as a journalist took over, and I simply asked for better access. Franklin became a trusted source, and soon I realized that accurate scoops were infinitely more satisfying than writing propaganda.

I recount all this ancient history because it helps explain why Jackson was hell-bent on having Andrew Young succeed him. Young would protect his legacy, bring stature to the office, and, most important, signal voters' confidence in keeping the mayor's job in Black hands. But a White state legislator, Sidney Marcus, jumped into the race, and polls showed him consolidating the White vote. There was no lack of irony in the way things stacked up. Young, with his experience on the world stage and his marquee charm, should have appealed to the White business establishment hungering for Atlanta to make good on its long-standing ambition of becoming an "international city." Marcus, a detail-oriented lawmaker who headed Fulton County's delegation in the state House of Representatives, enjoyed close friendships with his Black colleagues and promised the sort of attention to city services that would have benefited poor, predominantly Black neighborhoods.

But with voters largely sticking by their tribal loyalties, Young and Marcus finished the primary on October 6, 1981, in a near dead heat and headed for a runoff three weeks later. Shaken that he had corralled only about 10 percent of the White vote, Young shed his usually affable, diffident approach to campaigning and decided to play hardball. It was Jackson who did the dirty work for him. At a meeting of the Hungry Club Forum—a venerable forum for speeches directed to the Black community—at the Butler Street YMCA, Jackson took aim at Marcus's Black supporters in the legislature. "We are beginning to see shuffling and grinning around the camp of our opponent," he famously intoned, "by some of our former allies in the struggle." He referred to Marcus's backers as "Negroes" and accused them of racial "self-hatred" akin to the days of the plantation. For good measure, the mayor also unloaded on Abernathy and Williams for their endorsement of President Reagan the year before, calling them "slick-talking Negroes" hoping for "a scrap" from the table.

As it happened, I was at the state capitol that day, visiting with Billy McKinney, a veteran state representative who backed Marcus. A former Atlanta policeman known for his volcanic temper, and who still occasionally packed a pistol, McKinney got word of the speech and was profoundly hurt and angry. I recall being pretty certain he might have killed Jackson if he had encountered him that day. Another legislator in Marcus's camp, Doug Dean, told the newspaper, "I would rather him to call me a 'nigger.' That's what he meant."

It was ugly stuff, and I was stunned. At the time, I thought Jackson's speech was racist. Four decades later, I would not use that term, having come to believe that the word should be reserved for greater sins. Certainly the targets of Jackson's slander—whose ranks included Grace Hamilton, the first Black woman elected to the Georgia legislature, a figure of uncommon achievement in the long fight for civil rights—had reason to feel that race had been used as a cudgel against them, to make them feel shame that was completely undeserved. But I think I have learned that White people have little if any right to interfere in such matters. As it happened, Marcus's Black supporters could fend for themselves, and a few took to sporting T-shirts that said, "Grinning, Shuffling Negro," as if to say, sticks and stones.

Jackson defended himself at the time, saying he meant only to say that Black politicians who suggested that Marcus was more qualified than Young to be mayor were off base and trading in racial stereotypes. And if I wanted to be honest, I could find my own footprints in the path that led Jackson to do what he did.

In any case, Young won the election handily, there was a small measure of voting across racial lines after all, and Marcus accepted the outcome with the grace that characterized his entire political career.

THE NEWSROOM

When I went to work for the *Atlanta Constitution* in December 1972, there was exactly one Black reporter on the staff, a science writer named Chuck Bell. What I mostly remember about him was that he played a good game of chess. That summer I'd gotten captivated by the famous match between Bobby Fischer and Boris Spassky, and I fancied myself a decent player as well. We had some epic matches in a back room during slow news evenings.

I don't recall ever discussing race with Chuck, but I have a vivid memory of an incident that happened a few years later. In March 1975, the worst tornado in the city's history tore an eight-mile swath through Atlanta, peeling the roof off the governor's mansion and badly damaging the iconic Perry Homes housing project. Chuck and I were dispatched to an industrial section of town where we found a small factory reduced to a pile of bricks. We discovered a pair of boots sticking out of the rubble, the feet of one of three victims killed by the storm. It was the first corpse I'd ever encountered. As we took notes, a panicky, soot-stained

Black man came running past us out of the wreckage, and he shouted at Chuck, "Get outta my way, nigger!" I could feel a hot wave of embarrassment coming from Chuck as the crude epithet hung in the air. I told him I was sorry it had happened, and I may even have tried to explain away the moment by noting the circumstances. He did not want to talk about it. But what I clearly remember, all these years later, was how the fact that a White man had witnessed the encounter made it awful for Chuck in a way I could not fathom.

I've described how the front-page columns of Ralph McGill gave the *Constitution* a reputation for liberalism that was not entirely warranted. Through the 1950s, the paper ran a regular feature under the heading "Our Negro Community," giving snippets of news about Black folks as if they were a sideshow at the circus. In 1974, the sports department hired a teacher named Earnest Reese to cover athletics at the Atlanta University complex and ran stories with his photograph and a kicker that said "Reese Raps," making clear that a color line had been broken. That same year, the *Constitution* had the uncommon good sense to hire Alexis Scott, the granddaughter of the founder of the *Atlanta Daily World*, the nation's first Black-owned daily newspaper, and she has been a good friend of mine ever since. I still tease her about the day we "desegregated" Leb's, a downtown lunch spot best known for the hard line its proprietor, Charlie Lebedin, took against serving Black people during a sit-in campaign in 1964.

It was Alexis who gently undertook to further my education in some of the subtleties of race in Atlanta. One day she drove me out to Southwest High School, in the heart of the Black community's most prosperous section, where the students looked as preppy as my classmates at Andover. I told Alexis the boys resembled Pat Boone with a deep tan. One night she took me to a party at the home of Andy Young's brother, Walter, the well-to-do dentist. The point was to make sure I understood that Atlanta had a well-established Black middle class, that not all Black people lived in a ghetto, something I knew but perhaps not as well as I should have. In later years, she said something to me about race that had the ring of simple truth. "You think about race when it suits you," she said of White people. "We think about race every day because we have to."

Bit by bit, with no evident sense of urgency, the paper added to its slender roster of African American reporters, editors, and photographers. One of the most noteworthy arrivals, in 1979, was a fellow named Roger Witherspoon as our health and science writer. "The Spoon," as he was known to one and all, was given a weekly column at the same time I got promoted to chief political writer with a column of my own, and I felt a certain fraternal bond with him. Witherspoon got himself into trouble in the summer of 1979 with a column about the Peachtree Road Race that described in excruciating detail how a sixteen-year-old boy with cerebral palsy named Arnold endured agony while training for the race and then participating in it, his ungainly gait sending "shards of sensation—delayed, in his case, but very real nonetheless—through his system." The paper received calls and letters from readers knowledgeable about cerebral palsy who were highly skeptical that such a thing had happened.

Over the next two weeks, pressure mounted on Witherspoon to authenticate the column or admit it was fiction, and I recall an ugly undercurrent in the newsroom that made an issue of his race. Something very similar took place at the *Washington Post* two years later when Janet Cooke won a Pulitzer Prize for a feature story about an eight-year-old heroin addict named Jimmy, then admitted under duress that she had fabricated the tale and had to return the Pulitzer amid grumbles about affirmative action. I recall taking Witherspoon's side, counseling him to clear up the confusion and end the controversy. Two weeks after his initial column, he informed readers, "The story was largely apocryphal. Arnold is a real person, and his efforts to run in a mini-marathon—and his eventual success—were as described. But he did not run in Atlanta." To this day, journalists who worked at the *Constitution* at the time shake their heads over "largely apocryphal Arnold."

Unlike Janet Cooke, Witherspoon kept his job, probably because his transgression occurred in a column, not a news story. And I was glad he survived because a year later he pulled off a coup that made me appreciate having a clever Black journalist in the newsroom. William Shockley was a physicist, a brilliant electrical engineer who won a Nobel Prize for his work as part of the team at Bell Laboratories that invented the transistor. In the 1960s, Shockley turned his attention to genetics—a field in which he had no training or expertise—and began promoting a theory that Black people were less intelligent than White people and ought to be paid to submit to voluntary sterilization. Witherspoon conducted two hours of interviews with Shockley by phone and then had the satisfaction of writing a column that tore Shockley's beliefs to shreds. I remember thinking at the time that it was entirely fitting—heck, it was a hoot—to see Shockley outsmarted by a Black man.

Witherspoon's column was restrained, for the most part, but one paragraph infuriated Shockley and led him to file a libel suit. "The Shockley program," Witherspoon wrote, "was tried out in Germany during World War II when scientists under the direction of the government experimented on Jews and defectives in an effort to study genetic development." Today I believe the courts would dismiss Shockley's suit out of hand. He was not just a public figure, after all, but a publicity hound—at age seventy, he donated his sperm to a bank called the Repository for Germinal Choice, intended to spawn gifted children, and he welcomed news coverage as an opportunity to promote his ideas. An analogy to Hitler seemed perfectly fitting to me. After all, Nazi Germany's race laws were modeled on theories of eugenics developed in the United States. At the time, though, a federal judge let the case proceed to trial, which took place in 1984.

Proving that he was not, perhaps, quite as brilliant as he liked to think, Shockley gave an interview during the trial to the *Washington Post*, saying, "I'm enjoying myself . . . I like the attention," thereby undermining the very point of a libel suit, an injury to his reputation. And though his suit asked $1.25 million in damages, he also said he would be content "even if I didn't get one cent. My complaint is that people have not taken me seriously, you see." Guided by strict instructions from the judge, the jury found in Shockley's favor—but awarded him only a single dollar. It may seem at times that we have not made much progress on race over the years, but I think the outcome of the Shockley trial was a milestone of sorts. Twenty years earlier, a jury might well have awarded Shockley every dollar he asked plus punitive damages; twenty years later, I believe a jury would have returned a verdict totally in Witherspoon's favor.

While I have a vivid memory of Witherspoon, I barely knew another Black reporter, Nathan McCall, who came aboard in 1983, just after the morning *Constitution* and afternoon *Journal* combined their news operations. I took a year's sabbatical to escape the messiness of the merger, and when I returned in the autumn of 1983, McCall was working as a general assignment reporter. The truth is, I remember almost nothing about him, positive or negative. By that time, we had quite a few African American staffers, and I was unaware of any particular racial issues roiling the newsroom. We had come a long way from proclaiming a "City in Crisis" in 1975 during Mayor Maynard Jackson's first term, and were headed for a Pulitzer in 1989 for a series on redlining. I know how utterly naive it sounds when a White person professes not to see racism in the workplace, and I'm sure the inequities that afflicted society at large were operating at the *Journal-Constitution* as well, but what I mean is that by 1983 I thought I had a pretty good idea what a toxic racial atmosphere looked and sounded like, and I don't think we had one. The mid-1980s marked something of a relative calm in the choppy seas of race relations, a time beyond the violent battles of the 1960s and before Rodney King opened the lens on police violence against Black people.

In any case, I would not be scribbling these awkward sentences except that McCall wrote a bestseller, *Makes Me Wanna Holler*, a memoir that described his turbulent life, including the years he spent at the *Journal-Constitution*. "I stayed mad so much about one thing or another that I felt at times like I'd explode," he wrote, starting a chapter about his time at the newspaper. "I began to wonder how long I'd last in the white mainstream. The racism at work never ended. I could feel it in exchanges with whites all the time. It was always there, just below the surface, and it took a toll on me." Some of the experiences McCall described at the newspaper had the ring of harsh truth. Apparently one of his first assignments was covering a watermelon-eating contest at a county fair just outside Atlanta. "Of course," he wrote, "it set off alarms inside my head." Sure enough, two Black boys entered the competition and won handily, much to the amusement of the White farmers looking on. "All the while," McCall remembered, "I'm thinking, *Why me, Lord? Why do I have to see this shit?!*" On the police beat, McCall occasionally encountered sheriffs and other law enforcement officials in rural counties outside Atlanta who treated him badly.

I think there was a good deal of truth to McCall's assertion that White editors had a constricted view of the Black community. "The only stories the paper thoroughly covered about Blacks," he wrote, "related to protests, sports, discrimination, poverty, and crime."

But other sections of the book left me wondering if they were real. McCall describes arriving at a press conference in 1983 called by Hosea Williams, the civil rights legend, to announce a "Sweet Auburn" street festival meant to support efforts to revitalize Auburn Avenue, the main business thoroughfare of Atlanta's Black community. According to McCall, it was the first time they had met, and Williams subjected him to a withering, humiliating attack for working at the *Journal-Constitution*: "That's one of the most racist newspapers in the country," he quotes Williams saying, "and you down there Uncle Tommin' for them!? Don't you know I demonstrated against that paper so that black folks like you could get jobs there!? And y'all ain't done no better than the White folks at that paper. A bunch a' Uncle Toms. . . !" Based on my own experiences with Williams, and my friendship with him over the decades, I simply can't believe he would have treated McCall that way, especially over a routine story about Auburn Avenue.

And then there was his description of the White reporters he encountered in the men's room. "Standing next to a white dude at the urinal one day," he wrote, "I noticed him looking down at my penis. The first time it happened, I thought it was my imagination. Then, after I began to pay closer attention, I noticed that it happened often with a lot of different white guys in the men's room. They just *had* to look to see if the myths about black men's penis size were true." I remember reading that paragraph when McCall's book was published in 1994, and thinking, *Really? Are you kidding?*

The truly disturbing thing about McCall's book was his description of growing up in Norfolk, Virginia, as a hoodlum— not a juvenile delinquent, mind you, but a genuinely violent criminal who eventually served time in prison for armed robbery before turning his life around. His accounts of abusing women are difficult to read and impossible to forget. Writing a response at the time the book came out, Larry Conley, the African American editor of the *Journal-Constitution*'s Perspective section, explained his own misgivings about the book: "I was moved by the redemptive example of McCall's eventual success," he wrote, "but disappointed by the implication that the torturous path which led McCall into trouble was somehow unavoidable, an inevitable consequence of being a young black man in America." After all, Conley continued, his own circumstances had been more desperate than McCall's, yet he chose not to be a criminal. I had the same thought about McCall's choices—just not the standing to say so.

At the time I worked with him, McCall had yet to reveal his criminal record to the newspaper's management, and I recall him simply as a quiet fellow who kept to himself. I wonder if we might have had a closer relationship if I'd gotten to know him. On the other hand, he describes his later career, at the *Washington Post* and as a senior lecturer at Emory University, as being poisoned by the pervasive, unrelenting racism of the Whites he worked with, so perhaps not.

What I think I learned in the newsroom was that my Black colleagues labored under burdens that I was not as aware of as I should have been at the time, which is to say I should have been a better reporter and gotten the full story.

JULIAN BOND AND
JOHN LEWIS

I first laid eyes on Julian Bond, as did millions of other Americans, in the summer of 1968, when his name was placed in nomination for vice president during the Democratic National Convention in Chicago. Bond famously declined the nomination, as he was just twenty-eight years old at the time, too young to serve if elected. What made Bond's national debut so remarkable was the otherworldly cool he displayed, a sunny, urbane, supremely self-confident persona that belied the chaos taking place inside and outside the convention hall, launching him into celebrity.

Home from college that summer, I watched Bond on television and was transfixed. I remember telling my mother that in a time of tumult, I thought I had just seen someone I could believe in. It was the summer before my junior year, so I hope I may be forgiven for what turned out to be sophomoric thinking—but I'm quite sure I wasn't the only viewer who was captivated by him. If you had told me then that Bond's political career would never lift him beyond the Georgia legislature, I'm not sure I would have believed it. But then I got to know him, and I discovered an enigma.

In 1974, shortly after I went to work at the *Atlanta Constitution*, Bond was elected to the Georgia senate, after four terms in the Georgia house. In those days, reporters were allowed onto the floor of the senate chamber during recesses, and one day I wandered from the press section over to the empty desk next to Bond's. At his invitation, I sat down to join him for a chat. Bond was leaning back comfortably in his armchair, fingers steepled, eyes cast upward toward the visitors' gallery that ringed the room like the box seats in a theater, an expression of keen interest on his face. "Thinking great thoughts?" I asked. Bond got a gleam in his eye. "No," he said, adding, "in search of the elusive pooswah . . ." He was combing the gallery, that is, for female admirers and, well, of course I laughed. Bond's irreverence disarmed me. In a slightly more serious conversation around that time, Bond complained that the Watergate scandal had slammed the door on graft at the very moment Black politicians were finally poised to gain office and profit from it. As with his earlier comment, I was not at all certain he was joking.

I met John Lewis around the same time, when he was running the Voter Education Project in Atlanta, and he could not have presented a sharper contrast with Bond. Lewis was enshrined on a list of "Living Saints" in the Christmas 1975 issue of *TIME* magazine, and I found him to be as earnest and reverent as Bond was not. Lewis had staked his own claim to national fame on "Bloody Sunday" in 1965 when he helped lead the march in Selma, Alabama, that erupted in turmoil when state troopers tear-gassed and beat the marchers with nightsticks, leaving Lewis with a fractured skull. The televised images that day at the Edmund Pettus Bridge are credited with spurring passage of the Voting Rights Act. A follower of Dr. Martin Luther King Jr. and an ardent practitioner of nonviolence, Lewis spoke often of the "Beloved Community" without a trace of irony. I made the mistake of thinking he was moralistic, when in his own way, he, too, was an enigma.

The backgrounds of the two men were as different as their personalities. Bond grew up in rarefied circumstances, the son of a college president, accustomed to meeting distinguished visitors ranging from W. E. B. Du Bois to Alfred Einstein. "I have a picture of me," he once told an interviewer, with a trace of wonder, "sitting on Paul Robeson's knee while Robeson sings to me." At Lincoln University, in Pennsylvania, the family lived in a large white house that Bond thought resembled a Southern plantation manor. He attended the George School, a private Quaker prep school in Bucks County, Pennsylvania, where segregation seemed an alien concept.

Lewis, born in the same year as Bond, 1940, was one of ten children of sharecropper parents in rural Pike County, Alabama, where he picked cotton, did farm chores, and displayed an early bent toward evangelism by preaching to the chickens in his care. He would occasionally sneak away from his labors to take the bus to a ramshackle, segregated school, where the realities of "separate but equal" were obvious. "We had old broken-down buses," he recalled years later, "ragged books, a rundown building. White students had new buses, nice painted buildings, with the grounds kept up." From the soda fountain to the movie theater, Lewis was greeted with Jim Crow laws that made him a second-class citizen, or rather, not a citizen at all, because of the color of his skin.

Bond's epiphany about race came one day at the George School, when the dean called him into his office. Bond had begun dating a White girl, and he liked taking her into Philadelphia on weekend afternoons. The dean asked Bond not to wear his school jacket on those trips. "It was just as though he had slapped me across the face," Bond told *Life* magazine years later, the moment he realized he was "a Negro." When I first read the account, I thought it seemed a pretty mild way of encountering racial prejudice—and then on reflection I realized it must have been as hurtful in its way as any act of racism, impossible for a White person to fully understand, of course, but nonetheless a rude, cruel introduction to the realities of race in America.

True to their natures, Lewis and Bond took very different paths to activism in the civil rights movement. Lewis heard Martin Luther King Jr. preach on the radio in 1955, leading the Montgomery bus boycott, and became an immediate disciple of what he called "this holy, righteous cause." He worked his way through the American Baptist Seminary in Nashville, where he attended workshops on nonviolence and helped lead sit-ins, and in 1961 he became one of the original Freedom Riders. His physical courage became the stuff of legend, as he was arrested dozens of times, jailed, and beaten, but never once backed down.

Had he remained in the North, meanwhile, I'm not sure Bond would have become a "race man" at all. He yearned for a life of the mind, as a poet or writer, and once confessed, "I was fairly aimless, purposeless." But his father left Lincoln University to become the dean of education at Atlanta University in Atlanta, a citadel of Black higher education in the heart of the South, and Bond entered Morehouse College, where he was drawn inexorably into activism. He often told the story of a classmate having to browbeat him into helping organize the sit-in at Rich's department store that led to the arrest and jailing of Martin Luther

King Jr., one of the turning points of the era. It is easy to dismiss Bond as a dilettante, as many observers have done over the years, but I have always credited him with answering a challenge that did not easily suit him.

By the time I met them in the 1970s, Bond and Lewis were treading water in their careers. The harsh truth was that very few openings existed in Georgia for African Americans with ambition for high public office. In January 1977, Andrew Young vacated Atlanta's Fifth District congressional seat to become President Jimmy Carter's ambassador to the United Nations. To the surprise of many, Bond spurned the chance to run in the special election to replace him. Lewis did run and lost in a runoff against a White liberal, Wyche Fowler. Later that year, Bond hosted *Saturday Night Live*, suggesting that his celebrity counted for more in show business than in politics.

A low point for both men came in 1978, when Robert Scheer, a reporter with the *Los Angeles Times*, visited Atlanta to write a profile of the city. He set off with Bond and Lewis in search of Perry Homes, the giant housing project whose name had become a synonym for inner-city poverty. After an hour driving around, the two civil rights icons had to confess that they could not find the place, a failure that led some to tease them and others to remark how out of touch they had become. That Scheer's article turned out to be a savage indictment of Atlanta's image did not help.

Fast forward a decade, to 1986, when Fowler ran for the US Senate, once again vacating the Fifth District congressional seat. This time, fatefully, both Lewis and Bond announced their candidacies to replace him, setting in motion a contest that would define the remainder of their lives. As the *Journal-Constitution*'s political columnist at the time, I had a front-row seat covering the election and, as it happened, influencing the outcome. From the start, the smart money was on Bond to win. Polls showed him with a commanding two-to-one lead, and the city's Black political elite, led by former mayor Maynard Jackson, made no secret of their support for Bond. I remember Jackson's top adviser, the late David Franklin, telling me in a patronizing tone, "We'll have to find something for John when it's over." When Bond's team discovered that Lewis had spent $1,000 in campaign funds on elocution lessons, they snickered.

Looking back, I think Black voters favored Bond because they believed he would be a more articulate and visible champion of their politics than Lewis. Among Black leaders there was an undercurrent of resentment toward Lewis, who had loudly championed reform after winning an at-large seat on the Atlanta City Council. He was considered a pious busybody who broke an unwritten code by criticizing the ethics of other Black elected officials. Joseph Lowery, a colleague from the civil rights movement, once disparaged Lewis's image as a "living saint," saying, "I never heard anybody in the black community say that."

White voters, who made up 40 percent of the district's electorate, a significant chunk, had a mirror-reverse perspective. They liked Lewis's ethics and honesty, but many of them also figured he might not be quite as eloquent or effective as Bond in pursuing a liberal agenda, as much a plus to them as it was a minus among Black people.

After years covering Atlanta politics, I had concluded that the two races, Black and White, were like political parties, divided along partisan lines on a variety of issues but willing to switch sides if circumstances warranted. It was a mark of genuine racial comity, I thought, that the Fifth District seat was won and held by a Black man, Andrew Young, when its majority was White, and then by a White man, Wyche Fowler, after Black people gained the majority. Both were attractive politicians who courted and won votes from the other "party," and they did so by treading lightly on racial issues. The election of 1986, however, did not draw a strong White candidate, and as a result it put Bond and Lewis in the tricky position of trying to appeal to voters of both races without offending either. It would be an intramural affair with little to separate them on the issues. That is, it would be personal.

As the underdog, Lewis struck first. He gave a scathing interview to the *Washington Post*, lacing into Bond's reputation as a diffident and reluctant participant in the civil rights movement. "He's a friend," Lewis said, sharpening his knife, "but in the early years we had to bang on his door to wake him up and pull him out of bed to campaign." Bond, he added, "got out press releases, sent telegrams. I was on the front lines in Montgomery, Birmingham, Mississippi. He stayed back in Atlanta."

The saintly Lewis, it turned out, had a combative side, and it caught Bond off guard. "I don't believe John ever got me out of bed," he replied dryly, not seeming to know what to make of the attack. Lewis also took aim at Bond's celebrity, saying, "I'm not interested in representing the so-called beautiful people from Hollywood, New York, or Georgetown."

On primary night, August 12, 1986, Bond came within an eyelash of victory. Under Georgia law, a candidate had to take an outright majority of votes—50 percent plus one—to win, or else there would be a runoff between the top two finishers. Bond ended up with 47 percent, just short, and Lewis with 35. There were three weeks before the runoff, and Lewis went for broke.

There had been rumors in the Black community that Bond might have a drug problem, and Lewis made a show of taking a drug test, passing it, and then challenging Bond to follow suit. Bond replied with a mix of outrage—accusing Lewis of McCarthyism—and humor, saying in a televised debate, "President Reagan wants to give us 'Star Wars.' Mr. Lewis wants to give us 'Jar Wars.'" What he did not do was submit to a drug test.

I mentioned having contributed to the outcome. For decades, as a minority of the electorate in city elections and congressional races, the Black community had closely studied White candidates to decide who might best represent their interests (or in some cases, who might harm them least). In two mayoral elections, in 1957 and 1961, White voters had given slim majorities to the arch segregationist Lester Maddox, while Black voters threw their support to moderates, first William Hartsfield and then Ivan Allen Jr., who both won. In my column, I argued that White voters in the Fifth District now filled the role once played by Black voters and could swing the outcome if they voted in strong numbers. In the runoff, supporting Lewis by margins as high as ten-to-one in some precincts, they easily offset Bond's advantage among Black voters, and Lewis won in a dramatic upset. Years later, Lewis told me he thought my columns had turned the tide for him—a bit of flattery, I'm sure, but perhaps with a kernel of truth.

In any case, Lewis went on to win seventeen consecutive terms in Congress and to serve as a highly articulate champion of liberal politics and civil rights. Bond seemed at first to have weathered the storm. He was gracious in defeat. He continued to serve as president of the Atlanta chapter of the NAACP and was a draw on the national lecture circuit. In January 1987, PBS aired its acclaimed series on the civil rights movement, *Eyes on the Prize*, narrated by Bond, who sounded every bit the voice of authority on the subject.

But it was an illusion. Bond's life began to unravel on the evening of March 18, 1987, when his wife, Alice, discovered him riding in a car with a woman named Carmen Lopez, an accused cocaine dealer and, by subsequent accounts, Bond's supplier and mistress. Alice Bond followed the car to the driveway of Julian's mother's house, jumped out, and accosted Lopez, who promptly took off a shoe and hit Alice in the forehead with the stiletto heel, knocking her senseless. The next day, Alice Bond swore out a warrant against Lopez for battery. And then, for good measure, she walked into the narcotics office of the Atlanta Police Department and gave a lengthy, angry, highly incriminating tape-recorded interview to two detectives, accusing her husband of cocaine addiction and alleging that several high-ranking Atlanta political leaders and public figures were also drug abusers.

In some corners of the universe, Alice Bond's bombshell might have had a quieter outcome. Julian Bond might have gotten help for a drug problem. The police might have set up a sting and caught Carmen Lopez or others accused by Alice Bond of selling cocaine. The news might have been kept under wraps, sparing Bond public humiliation. But in Atlanta, the fault lines of race came immediately into play, with explosive results. Word of Alice Bond's statement leaked immediately throughout the city's police and political circles, reaching, among others, Julian Bond's campaign manager, Eugene Duffy, who now worked in city hall and told his boss, Mayor Andrew Young. Young's reaction was perfectly in character: he called Alice Bond and counseled her, as he put it, not to "do anything in a fit of emotion or anger that would do any damage to her or her family"—but it turned out to have volcanic consequences.

Mayor Young's phone call to Alice Bond took place around one o'clock on the afternoon of March 25, 1987, just as she was headed out the door for another meeting with the two narcotics detectives and two FBI agents they had brought in to the case. Unnerved that her statement had not remained confidential, Mrs. Bond went to the meeting and voiced sharp reservations about continuing to cooperate with the authorities. The investigation quickly unraveled. The two detectives and their supervisor were transferred out of the narcotics unit. A planned sting operation was called off. And then, not surprisingly, the whole mess was leaked to the media, erupting in banner headlines.

Bond was hounded by reporters and responded with outrage, calling them "vultures and hooligans" and denying, not very convincingly, that he used cocaine. He refused to discuss the details of what he called "a domestic affair, a quarrel between husband and wife." He admitted knowing Carmen Lopez but would not elaborate. He dismissed the narcotics detectives as "two white police officers who are well-known troublemakers."

A far more serious twist in the story was the sensational disclosure that Alice Bond had named Mayor Young himself as a cocaine user, and also his brother, Walter, a prominent dentist and friend of Julian Bond's. The new, ominous implication was that the mayor had intervened in the investigation to protect himself and his family, not the Bonds. The US attorney opened a grand jury investigation into Young's actions to determine if he had obstructed justice.

A full-blown scandal was unfolding, and race played a central role. Among the Black social and political elite—and among

White people who knew him, whose ranks included me—it was simply impossible to believe that Andy Young used cocaine. It was certainly impolitic of him to have called Mrs. Bond, but he freely admitted having done so and insisted his motives were innocent. He departed Atlanta the next day for a twenty-day trade mission to China, Japan, and London, unaware of the trouble brewing back home. In a telephone interview with the *Journal-Constitution* from Osaka, Japan, Young explained, "I said if she really had evidence, fine, but if she was just telling, passing rumors . . . she shouldn't do anything in a fit of emotion. I also told her that, personally, this could hurt her more than it hurt anybody else." He elaborated two days later, from London, saying, "I basically called a young lady that I thought might have been in distress. I didn't in any way attempt to interfere with her, but [was] simply trying to get her to take her time and think through with what she was doing and make sure it was what she wanted to do."

Well, no. In my view, the mayor thought Alice Bond was lighting the fuse on a time bomb that would blow up her husband and also the circle of elite Black leaders of which Young was very much a part. His call to her was highly injudicious. But was it criminal? My newspaper treated it that way. More than a dozen reporters were turned loose on the story, which soon shifted from the Bonds to a drumbeat of allegations that Mrs. Bond had named the mayor as a user of cocaine. I had trustworthy sources within the criminal justice system—I still can't reveal their names—who warned me that Mrs. Bond's accusation of the mayor was shaky at best and did not constitute reliable evidence that he had used drugs. I began to worry that the *Journal-Constitution* was unfairly portraying the mayor as a criminal. I tried to talk the editors into dialing back the coverage, but failed.

I felt strongly enough about the matter that I resigned. (I was hired the next day by CNN to cover the 1988 presidential race, so my martyrdom was short-lived.)

Eventually the tape recording of Alice Bond's interview was made public. What she said about the mayor was this: "Well, I don't know anything about Andy. I only know what I heard and I never seen Andy. I was told I saw and did see, but I don't remember seeing it." As I'd been warned, her statement barely qualified as hearsay and did not justify an accusation of drug use. On June 17, three long months after the affair began, US Attorney Robert Barr, a White Republican, announced that he would not pursue an indictment of Young or any other official for obstruction of justice, citing insufficient evidence. Just like that, the story was over.

In the aftermath, Young recovered quickly, completing his term as mayor. He took a leading hand in winning the centennial summer Olympics for Atlanta and remains a revered elder statesman to this day. John Lewis became a fixture in Congress. Julian Bond divorced his wife, moved away from Atlanta, and eventually restored some decorum to his life, serving as national chairman of the NAACP. When he died in 2015, the *Journal-Constitution*'s obituary barely mentioned the allegations of drug use.

What did we learn? I think the civil rights movement led many of us to see things as, well, black and white. Villains and heroes. In an earlier chapter, I tried to come to grips with bad actors, like Marvin Griffin, who were affable and charming. With Bond and Lewis, I learned that the good guys can have feet of clay. Bond succumbed to weakness, but that did not erase the many contributions he made to the cause. Lewis ran a nasty campaign but still had his saintly qualities. Atlanta's Black political establishment withstood the pressures of a scandal, showing that it had grown sturdier and more durable than many realized.

When he hosted *Saturday Night Live*, Bond acted in a skit he would come to regret. In a mock TV interview, cast regular Garrett Morris, dark-skinned and affecting an exaggerated street accent, wonders at length why White people assume they are more intelligent than Black people. Bond replies with a deadpan expression, "It's based on the fact that light-skinned blacks are smarter than dark-skinned blacks." Morris does a dramatic double-take and then responds with a drawn-out "Say *what*?" Funny, but as Bond later said, "I believe it treaded dangerously on the fine line between comedy and poor taste."

Actually, it crossed the line. But it serves as a razor-sharp reminder that some of the assumptions made about Bond and Lewis when their campaigns began—assumptions made by voters of both races, based on stereotypes—proved to be entirely wrong. That was the most important lesson of all.

PRESIDENTS

I was on the set of CNN one morning in August 1988, when a clip came in that showed Vice President George Bush, the Republican presidential nominee, referring to three of his grandchildren as "the little brown ones." These were the children of his son Jeb and Jeb's Mexican wife, Columba, and Bush was introducing them to his boss, President Ronald Reagan, with what seemed obvious affection, expressed in the clunky way he so often spoke.

Predictably, some critics accused Bush of insensitivity, or worse, and one of the anchors asked me if I thought the remark was racist. This was during my brief career as CNN's national political analyst, when I got paid to think aloud on the air. I don't remember exactly what I said, but the gist was, "For goodness' sake, *no!*" I did not think Bush harbored racist feelings about members of his own family. Bush defended himself with asperity, saying, "Those grandchildren are my pride and joy, and when I say pride, I mean it." The matter faded, though it is noteworthy that we still remember it three decades later.

I think of the "brown ones" whenever a public figure gets in trouble for saying or doing something that strikes a racial gong, and my point is that the media, and society at large, typically do a poor job of differentiating between the infelicitous and the genuinely ugly, between slips of the tongue and actual poison. In the summer of 2019, Joe Biden got himself raked over the coals for reminiscing about an earlier, more collegial time in the US Senate when he was able to get along with the late segregationist senators James Eastland of Mississippi and Herman Talmadge of Georgia. Speaking almost wistfully of Eastland, Biden said, "He never called me 'boy.' He always called me 'son.'" It was an odd thing to say, since "boy" was the cruel, demeaning way Southern White people of a certain generation spoke to Black men, not fellow US senators. It was tone-deaf, but hardly racist.

Any number of commentators seized on Biden's remarks as an opening to reflect on the wretchedness of the "seg" era, without pausing to note that Biden entered the Senate in 1973, when the heyday of massive resistance was over. Eastland and Talmadge were not peddling racist bile in those days, but even if they had been, was Biden to have refused to shake their hands? Conduct Senate business with them? Ride the basement tram with them? No. He would have been polite and cordial to fellow elected officials. Congress is gridlocked these days, but its members are still collegial and still form friendships across partisan lines. They just don't pass much legislation. In time, the debate over Biden narrowed to questions about his record on such issues as court-ordered busing for school desegregation, anti-crime legislation, and his handling of the confirmation hearings for Clarence Thomas—all perfectly legitimate topics with serious racial implications.

I am not arguing that we spend too much time on race but rather too little. Consider Trent Lott, the former senator from Mississippi. In 2002, as Senate Republican leader, he made what he thought was a jovial toast at the one hundredth birthday party for Strom Thurmond, the living embodiment of segregationist politics, who had run as the Dixiecrat candidate for president more than half a century earlier in 1948. "I want to say this about my state," Lott remarked. "When Strom Thurmond ran for president, we voted for him. We're proud of it. And if the rest of the country had followed our lead, we wouldn't have had all these problems over the years, either."

I thought then, as I do now, that Lott's comment fell somewhere beyond graceless humor but short of malevolent racial animus. What, one was forced to ask, were "all these problems" we might have avoided if Thurmond had been elected president instead of Harry Truman? I don't think Lott meant to argue seriously that the nation would be better off without the Civil Rights Act of 1964 or the Voting Rights Act of 1965 or other civil rights legislation that Thurmond and other Southern senators bitterly opposed—yet that was the punch line of the joke, and he paid a stiff price for it. He lost his job as party leader and a few years later resigned from the Senate. Lott was going for a chuckle, puffing up an old man, a spent force, on his centenary, but the joke was rooted in Thurmond's hateful heyday and thus out of bounds. It did not help that Lott hesitated before apologizing, and only half-heartedly at that.

Not long after the furor over Biden's comment on segregationist senators, a tape recording was released of a telephone conversation between President Richard Nixon and then-Governor Ronald Reagan of California, from October 1971, in which

Reagan referred to certain African diplomats at the United Nations as "monkeys" and observed, "They are still uncomfortable wearing shoes," a comment that earned him a laugh from Nixon. Reagan's calumny dropped swiftly from the news, mostly because he is dead, of course, but also in part because his daughter, Patty Davis, wrote an apology of uncommon grace in an op-ed article in the *Washington Post*, conceding the ugliness of her father's words.

The matter got me thinking about Reagan's uncanny ability to escape the consequences of a number of racially charged comments he made over the years, notably his speech embracing "states' rights" at the Neshoba County Fair in Mississippi, on August 3, 1980. Reagan launched his general election campaign against President Jimmy Carter seven miles from Philadelphia, Mississippi, where three civil rights workers—James Chaney, Andrew Goodman, and Michael Schwerner—had been abducted and murdered during 1964's "Freedom Summer" while trying to register Black people to vote. Carter was furious, thinking Reagan was using racial code language to appeal to Southern White voters who still took a dim view of civil rights. A few weeks later, in a famous speech at Ebenezer Baptist Church in Atlanta, standing in the King family's pulpit, Carter laced into Reagan for "the stirring of hate and the rebirth of code words," an attack that had very little effect on Reagan but led to a weeklong spate of articles and stories about Carter's alleged "mean streak" as a campaigner. Mary McGrory, the prominent syndicated columnist, wrote that Carter "is acting mean and fighting dirty," and Anthony Lewis of the *New York Times* assured his readers, "There is a mean streak in Carter the campaigner, and there always has been."

I had a small role in piling on. In 1980, I was writing a weekly column on politics in the *Atlanta Constitution*. It ran on Tuesdays, which happened to coincide with Carter's visit to Ebenezer. The president was greeted on the morning of September 16, 1980, with a headline that said, "Reagan Thinks He's Fighting a Gentleman!" I went on to liken Carter to a honey badger, a mean little animal that attacks by going for the groin. The White House press corps, traveling with Carter, was impressed with my apparent prescience when Carter went on the attack.

I had never warmed to Carter, finding his sanctimony as a man of faith to be at odds with what was indeed a mean streak in campaigning. At a press conference later that day, Carter stared daggers at me, much to the amusement of Burt Lance, his budget director, who stood at his side mugging at me, as if to say I was in trouble now. In the days that followed, it was mostly Black journalists, including Bob Herbert of the *New York Times*, who insisted that Reagan knew exactly what he was doing, rolling out the "Southern strategy" made famous by Richard Nixon, and it is a fact that Reagan carried every state of the Confederacy except Georgia later that fall. So I think I owe Carter an apology.

Four years later, on a hot October Monday in 1984, I remember standing with my colleague Bill Shipp in a throng of about ten thousand gathered in front of city hall in Macon, Georgia, for a Reagan reelection rally. Shipp had been my boss years earlier when he was the *Constitution*'s city editor and I was a cub reporter, and he had been a mentor to me ever since. Reagan started things off by proclaiming, "The South shall rise again!" There is no way of telling what anyone means, exactly, by this old chestnut, except that it is rarely entirely innocent. Shipp took a jaundiced view:

"The president of the United States," he wrote later, "obviously believes Georgians are still a gaggle of unreconstructed Rebel yahoos." Plainly irked, he added, "It means Negroes in white coats serving iced tea on the lawn and happy darkies singing as they chop cotton in the fields."

Before his speech got too heavy, Reagan veered off to denounce Democrats as big spenders, which got a big hand from the audience, and he advocated having a line-item veto in the federal budget, which would permit presidents to cherry-pick expenditures to axe. Then, adopting that famous conspiratorial whisper he had perfected, Reagan added, "Do you know that was favored by a leader named Jefferson Davis?" In the utter, absolute silence that followed, Shipp snorted and explained the president's miscalculation to me: First, few Southerners revere the name of Jefferson Davis. The heroes of the Confederacy were the generals, starting with Robert E. Lee, and not the politicians. To the extent that any Southern officeholder commanded affection in Georgia, it was the Confederate vice president, Alexander Stephens, a Georgian, and not Davis, who hailed from Mississippi and was considered an inept leader. And finally, this was a festive midday crowd, not a gathering of Civil War scholars. Shipp doubted that one in a hundred of them knew—or cared—that the Confederate Constitution had the line-item veto.

Reagan was trying to pander to a Southern audience without knowing enough to bring it off—a misdemeanor, in my book, not a felony, but I understood why Shipp was offended. He was a native Southerner, and I was just an adoptive one. He resented Reagan's assumption that all White Southerners think alike, in retrograde lockstep, and I didn't blame him.

My biggest challenge in refereeing the culpability of presidential candidates in matters of race came with George Bush in 1988—not the little brown ones but a large Black one: Willie Horton. It is commonly believed today that the Bush campaign engaged in race-baiting by exploiting the case of Willie Horton to smear the Democratic nominee, Governor Michael Dukakis of Massachusetts, as a coddler of criminals in general and of one criminal in particular who sported an Afro and beard and looked menacing.

The truth is a lot more complicated. Horton was a convicted murderer serving a life sentence in Massachusetts when he became eligible for a weekend furlough. He escaped and later raped a woman and stabbed her companion in a brutal home invasion. The case gained prominence when a Massachusetts newspaper, the *Lawrence Eagle-Tribune*, began a series of 175 critical articles about the furlough program that won a Pulitzer Prize. The staid *Reader's Digest* weighed in with an article called "Getting Away with Murder." The first politician to use the issue against Dukakis was a fellow candidate for the Democratic presidential nomination, Senator Al Gore of Tennessee, well before Bush seized on it.

The issues in the Horton case were fair game for a debate about criminal justice. In the 1980s, most states had similar weekend release programs, as did the federal government. The system in Massachusetts was started by a Republican governor. But Dukakis had taken a very liberal approach to furloughs. When the Massachusetts legislature passed a bill excluding first-degree murderers from eligibility, Dukakis vetoed it, saying it would "cut the heart out of efforts at inmate rehabilitation." He had legitimate exposure to political attack. But it was the nature of the attack, of course, that made it so controversial.

A political action committee with ties to the Bush campaign crafted a thirty-second television ad called "Weekend Passes" that recounted the details of Horton's crimes, labeled Dukakis soft on crime, and famously used a mugshot of Horton that made him look like a monster. The Bush campaign admitted taking a hand in the commercial. Roger Ailes openly bragged, "The only question is whether we depict Willie Horton with a knife in his hand, or without it." Bush's campaign manager, Lee Atwater, joked about turning Horton into Dukakis's running mate. Not surprisingly, the ad is remembered as racist. On his deathbed, Atwater repented and apologized for it.

But the Willie Horton ad ran only a handful of times, on independent cable stations in a single market, Washington, DC, and was seen by hundreds, not thousands of voters. What made it such a bombshell was the mainstream media—the newspapers, magazines, and TV networks—that showed the offending mugshot over and over again in stories, editorials, and commentaries, reaching millions of voters, until it became an inescapable totem of the campaign.

The official Bush campaign ran a very different TV ad called "Revolving Door" that depicted a turnstile releasing prisoners to freedom beyond bars. I recall criticizing the ad on CNN one night, saying it played on racial fears by showing Black criminals filing out of prison. The next day I had a call from Lee Atwater chiding me. The ad showed exactly two Black prisoners, he insisted, and all the rest were White. And it did not even mention Willie Horton. I took a copy of the ad to an editing bay and ran it over and over in slow motion. Sure enough, exactly two of the prisoners in the ad were Black, the rest all White. I apologized and corrected my further commentaries.

In my view, Dukakis was not the real victim of the ads. He probably did more damage to himself riding around in a tank looking like Snoopy, the iconic image of the campaign, than he suffered from the Horton affair. He was a wooden candidate and a cold fish. I remember the CNN debate when our lead political anchor, Bernard Shaw, directed the first question to Dukakis and asked if he would continue to oppose the death penalty if his wife, Kitty, were raped and murdered. Dukakis replied with otherworldly dispassion, reciting by rote the reasons for his opposition to capital punishment, while metaphorically, in the minds of viewers, poor Kitty Dukakis's ravaged corpse lay cooling nearby on the stage.

The lasting damage from the Horton affair was not so much to Dukakis as to our enduring struggle to come to grips with race. And it was inflicted mostly by the photograph of Horton, not the debate about the merits of prisoner furloughs. Looking back, it is striking to me that the searing toxicity of Horton's mugshot was not immediately recognized and denounced. But I think I understand why. No one, including me, wanted to say that a photograph of a Black man was incendiary, in and of itself. No one wanted to say Willie Horton was a scary-looking dude.

On October 24, 1988, just two weeks before Election Day, the *New York Times* ran a front-page story under the headline "Foes Accuse Bush Campaign of Inflaming Racial Tension." Even then, the Dukakis camp pulled its punches. Jesse Jackson held a press conference and accused the Bush campaign of sending "a number of rather ugly race-conscious signals." Dukakis's running mate, Senator Lloyd Bentsen of Texas, appeared on *This Week* on ABC. Asked if the prison furlough issue had a racial element, he replied delicately, "When you add it up, I think there is, and that's unfortunate."

Dukakis's campaign manager, Susan Estrich, was more direct. "There is no stronger metaphor for racial hatred in our country than the black man raping the white woman," she told the *Times*. "If you were going to run a campaign of fear and smear and appeal to racial hatred you could not have picked a better case to use than this one." But I think she missed the point too. No account that I can find specified the race of Horton's victims. No focus was placed on them, and their names are long since forgotten. The racial angle, plain and simple, was Willie Horton alone.

As it happened, the mugshot of Horton was taken after he spent time in solitary confinement recovering from surgeries for the gunshot wounds he received during his capture after the home invasion. He was fully aware of how he looked. Years later, in a fine irony, he told an interviewer, "I would have been scared of me too."

In his own patrician way, Bush could be as mean a campaigner as Jimmy Carter. There is no question in my mind that he and his advisers knew exactly what the original Horton ad would convey. They also likely understood that the media would do their dirty work for them, broadcasting the image of Horton far and wide, endlessly, for free. For our part, we in the media rarely paused to think if our stories or commentaries might have an effect opposite of what we liked to imagine. We tut-tutted in disapproval while metastasizing the message. And the cost was substantial. In the years after the election, fearful of seeming soft on crime, both parties in Congress supported legislation that led to heavier incarceration and longer sentences, decisions that are sharply questioned today.

Thirty years later, Joe Biden came under fire from some of his Democratic opponents for having championed harsh criminal laws during his Senate career. And they had a point. As Biden explained in 1989, "One of my objectives, quite frankly, is to lock Willie Horton up in jail."

I'd say he got the message.

SANDERS

On a sultry Saturday night in May 2014, my wife and I ventured to Broadway and took our seats in the second row of the Neil Simon Theatre to watch the hit play *All the Way*, starring Bryan Cranston as Lyndon B. Johnson. The title referred to Johnson's election slogan, "All the Way with LBJ," and the play covered events in the year after President Kennedy's assassination, in which Johnson pushed through passage of the Civil Rights Act and set about campaigning for a full term of his own.

As I paged through the *Playbill*, I was surprised to see that former Governor Carl Sanders of Georgia was listed in the cast of characters. I knew Sanders well, as did every political journalist in Georgia. He'd been elected in 1962 on a platform that was considered progressive for its time: "I'm a segregationist," he said, "but not a damned fool," a distinction everyone understood. He had aligned himself with the Coca-Cola Company and other big-business interests in Atlanta, and he spurned the gestures of massive resistance that scarred the reputations of Birmingham and other Southern cities. He was a staunch supporter of Johnson's campaign in 1964 but had not, so far as I could recall, done anything that would merit inclusion in a drama.

On the stage, playwright Robert Schenkkan conjured up a nighttime scene in the White House where a weary Johnson, in bed in his pajamas, reluctantly accepts a phone call from Sanders. The governor is calling from the Democratic convention in Atlantic City, where he heads the Georgia delegation. The subject is a highly convoluted plan Johnson had concocted to mollify a protest group, the integrationist Mississippi Freedom Democratic Party, by seating two of its members as at-large delegates. In the fraught political atmosphere of the time, Johnson's idea threatened to trigger a walkout by the all-White delegations from the Southern states. An anxious Sanders admonishes Johnson, "Mr. President! You can't give those people two seats! It makes it look like the niggers have taken over the convention!" He adds, "Me and my delegation might just walk out ourselves and God only knows who might follow us. The whole South might bolt!"

Johnson receives this spiteful news with exasperation and delivers an explosive response: "You listen to me! You need to make up your mind, once and for all, just what kind of Christian you are. Are you a once-a-week fella, or do you hold the Word in your heart? What kind of politician are you? You just out for yourself, or do you want to make a better life for all the people of Georgia? And what kind of man are you? You got the balls to do what you know is right? Or do you just slink away?"

Hearing this exchange startled and disturbed me because it seemed totally out of character for Sanders, and because it attributed to Johnson a passionate, eloquent, consequential diatribe about race and civil rights that I had never seen quoted anywhere before.

Barred by state law from seeking a second consecutive term in 1966, Sanders had watched in embarrassment as Lester Maddox succeeded him. Leaving office, he became a highly successful lawyer and took a hand in bringing major league sports to Atlanta. Then, in 1970, Sanders earned a footnote in national history by facing off for a second term against Jimmy Carter, who tagged him with the nickname "Cufflinks Carl" and ran an ugly campaign meant to appeal to the most backward elements of the Georgia electorate. Calling himself "basically a redneck," Carter vowed to invite George Wallace to visit Georgia—something Sanders had pointedly refused to do—and aligned himself with Maddox. The low point came when a Carter aide attended a Ku Klux Klan rally and passed out photographs of Sanders being doused with champagne by Lou Hudson, a star Black player on the Atlanta Hawks basketball team.

Only after winning did Carter switch tacks, vowing to be a "New South" governor. "I say to you quite frankly that the time for racial discrimination is over," Carter famously announced at his inaugural, leaving many of his supporters flabbergasted. Soon he was on the cover of *TIME*. Sanders returned to private life and never again ran for office.

I left the theater and returned to Atlanta determined to track down the quotation from Johnson and resolve the contradiction between the Sanders I thought I knew and the Sanders depicted on the stage. I did some digging and learned that tape recordings Johnson made of his phone calls in the Oval Office had been declassified and were housed at the Miller Center at the University of Virginia. The once-secret tapes were now easily accessible, and I soon found myself at my desktop computer in Atlanta, eavesdropping in utter fascination on a series of actual conversations between Johnson and Sanders on August 25 and 26, 1964.

This much was true: the president was trying to engineer what he called a "pure Johnson move" that would recognize two members of the Mississippi Freedom group as general delegates to the convention, while simultaneously seating the all-White official delegations from that state and Alabama. Sanders and Texas governor John Connally, the president's closest political ally, were on the convention floor in Atlantic City trying to mediate a peaceful resolution of what threatened to turn into a crisis. The pivotal call from Sanders came on Wednesday, August 26, 1964, the third day of the convention, and it went through to the Oval Office, not the president's bedroom. Warning of impending "complete havoc," Sanders tells Johnson, "I honestly believe you're gonna have a wholesale walkout from the South."

Johnson objects that seating two at-large delegates is a token gesture. "I don't see," he says, "how it hurts anybody—" Sanders interrupts him, "I know what it looks like to the South. And I'm just telling you because you want me to tell you the truth. It looks like we're turning the Democratic Party over to the Nigras." That was the kernel that inspired the playwright, and it is certainly jarring enough, but it was meant as a cold-eyed assessment of the political situation and not a statement of Sanders's own beliefs.

Sanders did not threaten to walk out with the Georgia delegation, and Johnson's challenge of his faith and manhood in the play is a complete fabrication. What Johnson actually said was, "Two niggers can't take over anything, Carl."

One reason Cranston won a Tony Award for his performance was his skill at capturing the almost histrionic way Johnson had of emoting, one moment wheedling and cajoling, the next wallowing in self-pity, the next bellowing in righteous anger—exactly as he does on the tapes. Describing his delegate plan, he tells Sanders, "It's just a pure, symbolic, pussyfootin' thing, to try to keep from splittin' the party like Goldwater'd like to see it split," adding, "all it does is just stop the agony and the pain and the bad publicity of three damn days here on television." Speaking of Mississippi and Alabama, he snaps, "They've caused more goddamn trouble and done less for it than any two states I ever heard of in my life." In a later conversation with Sanders and Connally, Johnson says, "Both of you are young and modern and effective, and I'm a poor old man here that's got a government falling [in] on me."

There are flashes of Johnson's anger toward the Southern White officials who had blocked civil rights for their Black citizens, not in the form of a cloudburst on religion and courage as heard in Schenkkan's play but in Johnson's actual, idiosyncratic words: "They got to let 'em vote, and they got to let 'em shave, and they got to let 'em eat!" (I thought, *"Shave"? Where in the world did that come from?* But those were the sentiments that buoyed Johnson as he secured passage of the Voting Rights Act the next year.) Rather than savage Sanders, the president actually commends him for voting reforms in Georgia.

So what are we to make of this twist in the historical record? My instinct was to write an op-ed for my old newspaper, the *Atlanta Journal-Constitution*, setting things straight. But it was awkward. There was the matter of the words "Nigra" and "nigger," now toxic, but in the 1960s a point of careful distinction. Then, as now, "nigger" was ugly, but White families in the South considered it a matter of breeding and politeness to say "Nigra," an accented form of Negro, instead. In the play, Sanders used the word "nigger," but on the tapes he plainly says "Nigra," and it is the president who uses "nigger." Parsing these distinctions in the newspaper did not strike me as doing much of a favor for Sanders. I thought of an old story from journalism school about a politician who demands a retraction when his local newspaper said he would steal a red-hot stove. Fine, the editor said—and ran a correction saying the politician would *not* steal a red-hot stove.

In November 2014, Sanders died. Abashed at having let the matter drift, I belatedly offered an op-ed article to the *Journal-Constitution*, making the points I've cited. In a fine irony, I ran straight into the dicey question of whether the word "niggers" could be used at all in the newspaper, no matter the context. I quoted verbatim from the play, with Sanders saying, "It makes it look like the niggers have taken over the convention." I thought the reason for including the word was obvious: it had been uttered on the stage of a Broadway theater in a play that won the Tony Award for best drama, and it was necessary, I thought, to explain why it was such a disservice to Sanders to suggest he had used the word when he had not. But the editors were adamant. In my op-ed piece the word was rendered as "n-----s" and "the N-word."

I was unhappy about the use of these euphemisms—not least because I believe they force a reader to utter the word in his or her own voice in the mind's ear, something I find more distasteful than encountering it directly—but who was I to say? By 2014, the word was too toxic to be used in a family newspaper. I was left to ruminate on the fact that the president had actually used the word in 1964, the year he used every political trick in his magician's bag to secure passage of the greatest civil rights legislation since Emancipation.

SILENT SAM

Pretend for a moment you've been transported back in time, more than a century, to a spring day in June 1913. You've come to the campus of the University of North Carolina, in Chapel Hill, for the dedication of a memorial to the Confederacy. Under overcast skies, on the rolling lawns surrounding Gerrard Hall, a large crowd of about a thousand has gathered in formal attire, the women wearing bonnets, to observe the regular commencement ceremony along with the unveiling of a statue dedicated to the students of an earlier generation who left school to fight in the Civil War.

A number of dignitaries make remarks, led by Governor Locke Craig, but the honor of introducing the statue falls to Mrs. H. A. London of the United Daughters of the Confederacy, the chair of the group's monument fund committee. One of her comments strikes an uncommonly conciliatory tone. "In honoring the memory of our Confederate heroes," she says, "we must not be misunderstood as having in our hearts any hatred of those who wore the blue." In the decades since the war's end, many aging veterans from both sides have discovered a fraternal bond, and even hold occasional joint reunions. Regional reconciliation has been a common theme ever since Henry Grady proclaimed a New South.

The final speaker is a familiar figure. His name is Julian Carr, one of North Carolina's richest men and the statue's largest donor. In 1864, at age eighteen, he left the university to enlist in the Confederate Army, where he served as a private and was present at Appomattox when the war ended. In the half century since, his devotion to the "Sacred Cause," as he calls it, has bordered on obsession. He dresses in uniform and likes to be called "General." His speech is a flowery tribute to the valor of Confederate soldiers. "Their sublime courage," he intones, "has thrown upon the sky of Dixie a picture so bright and beautiful that neither defeat, nor disaster, nor oppression, nor smoke, nor fire, nor devastation, nor desolation, dire and calamitous . . . has been able to mar or blemish it."

Carr rattles on at length, and your attention begins to slip, when suddenly he says he would like to tell a personal story. "One hundred yards from where we stand," he begins, "less than ninety days perhaps after my return from Appomattox, I horse-whipped a Negro wench until her skirts hung in shreds, because upon the streets of this quiet village she had publicly insulted and maligned a Southern lady."

You snap to attention. What in the world did he just say? He continues, recounting how the Black woman "rushed for protection to these university buildings, where was stationed a garrison of a hundred federal soldiers. I performed the pleasing duty in the immediate presence of the entire garrison." Carr finishes his story by saying he spent the next month sleeping with a double-barrel shotgun under his pillow. And then, as if he has said nothing of particular moment, he concludes his speech with more words of praise for the Confederacy.

He leaves you, head spinning, with several pressing, unanswered questions. What did this Black woman say or do to occasion such a brutal beating? Why did Carr take it upon himself to administer it? Why did a garrison of federal troops, posted as a force of occupation and charged with protecting the peace, stand by idly while a freedwoman was assaulted? Why did Carr fear retribution? And from whom?

I have conjured up this exercise in time travel because the speech Julian Carr made on that day in 1913 lay dormant for almost a century, until its rediscovery in modern times fueled several years of protests that culminated with the toppling of the monument, called Silent Sam, in 2018 under cover of darkness, one of the most dramatic episodes in the South's ongoing struggle to come to grips with symbols of the Confederacy.

In my undergraduate days at Chapel Hill, in the late 1960s, most of us considered Silent Sam a benign landmark. His nickname referred to a hoary campus witticism that he fired his gun only when a virgin walked by. Later, military experts noticed that the sculptor, a Canadian, had rendered the statue without a cartridge box so that Sam was effectively unarmed, and it became a matter of lore that he was meant to convey a passive, even pacifist, message. The statue drew a handful of protests back then, but it was more often a target of vandalism by students at rival universities during athletic contests. Given the heightened debate over Confederate memorials in recent years, it seems possible to me that the statue might have come down eventually in any case, but Carr's speech galvanized the issue, and I think it focused attention where it belongs—on the state of affairs in 1913.

I like to imagine that many in the audience at the statue's unveiling listened to Carr's violent account with discomfort or even shock. But perhaps not. I find no reference to it in newspaper accounts or the *Alumni Review*, which gave lengthy coverage to the ceremony. While the whipping story is far and away the most arresting part of the speech, other aspects are also jarring. Carr lamented that the current generation, nearly fifty years removed from the war, "scarcely takes note of what the Confederate soldier meant to the welfare of the Anglo Saxon race during the four years immediately succeeding the war," a not very oblique reference to the rise of the Ku Klux Klan, whose reign of terror helped restore the old order. Because of the Klan, Carr said, "the purest strain of the Anglo Saxon is to be found in the thirteen Southern states—Praise God."

As smoking guns go, Carr's speech is hard to beat, and the point it brings home to me is how fully and completely the idea of White supremacy had taken root by the early 1900s. Those who oppose the removal of Confederate symbols often deplore "presentism," the application of evolved standards when judging events of the past. Very well. There is nothing remotely acceptable about the plight of Black Americans in 1913. Silent Sam was unveiled into a society that was not just segregated but saturated with the idea that African Americans were an inferior race. Minstrelsy, blackface, and caricature inflicted savage mockery. Lynching and race riots inflicted worse—death. For a brilliant, utterly dismaying catalogue of the horrors visited on Black Americans from the end of Reconstruction in 1877 to the early decades of the 1900s, in the North as well as the South, one may read Henry Louis Gates Jr.'s book, *Stony the Road*, but it requires a strong stomach.

And remarkably, things were about to get *worse*. It was another loud campus protest, this one at Princeton University in the autumn of 2015, that focused fresh attention on Woodrow Wilson's record on race, which in a word was deplorable. Wilson was a virulent racist. He believed, as he once said, that Black people were "an ignorant and inferior race." He asserted that slaves were "happy and well cared for." He wrote a history of the American people that praised the Ku Klux Klan, saw to it as president of Princeton that no Black students were admitted on his watch, and assembled an all-White administration when he was governor of New Jersey from 1911 to 1913. Then, as president, he took steps meant to undo the modest but hard-earned gains of Black people who worked in the federal government.

Wilson allowed members of his cabinet to impose segregation in several departments and agencies of the government, including the Treasury and Interior Departments, the navy, and the post office. Black people who had taken and passed the civil service test were demoted. Offices were strictly divided by race. Black people were relegated to separate dining room tables, dressing rooms, lockers, and toilets. Black leaders were appalled, not least because Wilson, who held himself out as a progressive, had campaigned for their votes.

William Monroe Trotter, a prominent civil rights activist who had supported Wilson, sought a face-to-face meeting. On November 12, 1914, he and a small group of Black leaders were shown into the Oval Office. It did not go well. A graduate of Harvard, the first African American to earn a Phi Beta Kappa key there, Trotter was no shrinking violet. He read a prepared statement listing the federal offices that had been segregated and then posed a stinging question that mocked Wilson's campaign platform: "Have you a 'New Freedom' for white Americans," he demanded, "and a 'New Slavery' for your Afro-American citizens? God forbid!"

Wilson protested that separating the races was a benign practice meant to "prevent any kind of friction between the white employees and the Negro employees," but Trotter would have none of it. He called segregation a "humiliation" that "creates in the minds of others [the idea] that there is something the matter with us—that we are not their equals, that we are not their brothers, that we are so different that we cannot work at a desk next to them, that we cannot eat at table beside them, that we cannot go into the dressing room where they go, that we cannot use a locker beside them." Trotter's lament went on, his wounded passion obvious.

But the president, a notoriously prickly man, had had enough. "Your tone, sir, offends me," he told Trotter, and he warned the group that if it were ever to return, it would have to be with a different leader. "You have spoiled the whole cause for which you came," he warned Trotter. Taken aback, Trotter softened his tone, saying he was merely "pleading for simple justice," and apologized if he had been misunderstood. But it was too late. Wilson dismissed the group and had them escorted from the White House. The *New York Press* captured the essence of the encounter in its headline the next day: "Wilson Rebukes Negro Who 'Talks Up' to Him."

Perhaps we should not be surprised that a few months later, in 1915, Wilson arranged a screening of *Birth of a Nation*, the infamous motion picture that paid homage to the Ku Klux Klan, at the White House.

Is it unfair to dig up these ugly shards of nearly forgotten history? I don't think so. Our standards evolve because we examine history, not ignore it. But we face a very real, unresolved question about what to do with the burdensome monuments, memorials, and symbols that survive today. Should we tear them down? At times the impulse to disinfect the past can seem almost laughably obscure. Consider the decision by Harvard Law School in 2016 to retire its shield because it depicted three sheaves of wheat, a symbol taken from the crest of the Royall family, slave owners who helped endow the law school's first professorship. That struck me as almost a parody of political correctness. But the toppling of Silent Sam was serious business. It triggered a great deal of collateral damage, including the resignation of the university's chancellor, amid a bitter debate over an act of civil disobedience. When I wrote the first draft of this chapter, Princeton still had its Woodrow Wilson School of Public and International Affairs, and I predicted—quite incorrectly, as it happened—that it would remain, because presidents are difficult to sandblast off anything. Well, no, off it came, an indication just how toxic Wilson's name had become.

One school of thought holds that we should leave Confederate memorials standing in place, but with greatly enhanced explanations—in panels, markers, tablets, and interactive media—that fully describe the circumstances that led to their creation. An estimated 90 percent of the Confederate monuments in the South date from 1890 or later and were erected as part of the "Lost Cause" campaign led by the United Daughters of the Confederacy, meant to clothe their ancestors in nobler raiment than fighting for the preservation of a slave economy. Annette Gordon-Reed, the African American scholar who demonstrated that

Thomas Jefferson fathered a child by Sally Hemmings, opposed junking the Harvard Law School shield. "People should *have* to think about slavery when they think of the Harvard shield," she argued, and they should do so from the perspective of those enslaved, not merely the owners. Fair enough.

But the truth, I fear, is that it is only the fierce protests and efforts to tear down the monuments that fully publicize their histories. Leaving them in place, even with complete displays of their provenance, will not provoke the same level of reexamination as a loud and contentious public debate. Taken to its logical conclusion, however, removing them is no better because sooner or later there will be no symbols left to ignite our curiosity. Perhaps hypocrisy will have to do. Tear some down, leave some standing, and accept that only an ongoing debate will create a path to better understanding. A few sensible standards can certainly be adopted. A Confederate monument standing on the grounds of a courthouse, say, or a state capitol or a public university campus carries a suggestion of government approval and probably merits removal to a history center or museum.

I suspect we will keep muddling along, with random paroxysms causing contention but also opening the curtain on our past. One footnote from Julian Carr's speech, which I have not seen reported elsewhere, describes an occasion in 1909, four years earlier, when the university decided to confer diplomas on all of its students who served in the Confederate Army. Wilson, then the president of Princeton, traveled south to Chapel Hill to give a speech about Robert E. Lee, and while there he agreed to present the diplomas. His talk is remembered for its lavish praise of Lee and for his comment that he felt more at home in the South, where he was born and reared, than anywhere else in the country.

As it happened, very few of the veterans were still alive and only one attended—Carr, wearing his uniform. "At the dinner, later in the day," he recounted, "Professor Wilson greeted me with the remark that nothing had so much touched and warmed his heart as the sight of that Confederate uniform."

RECONSTRUCTION

My path to a clearer understanding of Reconstruction—and its collapse—began in Montana, of all places, our second home for more than two decades. Like most newcomers, I was drawn to the Battle of the Little Bighorn, visiting the site and studying the military disaster that befell George Armstrong Custer in 1876. But over time my focus shifted to a conflict that took place a year later, the Nez Perce War, which I believe was far more consequential. In brief, the Nez Perce were ordered onto a reservation a fraction the size of their ancestral lands, and rather than obey, a large faction of their entire nation—a thousand men, women, and children—took flight in 1877 hoping to reach sanctuary in Canada.

The man tasked with catching the Nez Perce, Oliver Otis Howard, is the protagonist of my story. On paper at least, Howard seems the embodiment of an American hero. A native of Maine, he graduated near the top of his class from West Point. He served with distinction during the Civil War, rising to the rank of major general. He lost an arm at the Battle of Fair Oaks and was awarded the congressional Medal of Honor for his service and sacrifice. His nickname, the "Christian General," referred to his evangelical faith. He believed in abolition, abstinence, and clean living.

Most notably, Howard served as the first head of the Freedmen's Bureau, where I will argue that his intentions were good, but his flawed actions in dealing with President Andrew Johnson exemplified the failure of Reconstruction to clear a path forward for the four million slaves emancipated during the Civil War.

In the West, years later, General Howard tried to talk the Nez Perce into accepting life on the reservation. When they refused and fled, Howard gave chase. His surprising ineptitude as a commander soon inspired the American Indians to give him a scornful nickname—"General Day After Tomorrow." Howard, it turned out, was not by nature an aggressive man, not a born warrior like a Lee, Grant, or Sherman. The Nez Perce led Howard on a seventeen-hundred-mile chase through the Rocky Mountains, including a dramatic detour through the fledgling Yellowstone National Park, and engaged the US military in thirteen skirmishes and battles, not once losing an encounter.

In the end, Howard left it to another soldier, General Nelson A. Miles, to catch the Nez Perce in the Bears Paw Mountains of north central Montana, just forty miles from the Canadian border, where they were forced to surrender. The words of their leader, Chief Joseph, were famously recorded as, "Hear me, my chiefs. I am tired. My heart is sick and sad. From where the sun now stands I will fight no more forever"—a lament that has entered American history as among the saddest words ever uttered. A man of immense charisma, Chief Joseph eventually became a revered figure—sometimes I think every middle school west of the Mississippi River is named for him—while General Howard was reduced to explaining away his laggard behavior and trying to salvage his tattered reputation. I began to wonder if Howard's shortcomings had also affected his performance at the Freedmen's Bureau.

Otis Howard—he was called by his middle name—was born in Leeds, Maine, in 1830, the first child of parents who worked an eighty-acre farm and bred and trained horses. In his autobiography, Howard recalls that when he was about five, his father brought home a young Black boy who lived with the family for the next four years. Howard does not explain the circumstances of this arrangement, but he credits his friendship with the young man for giving him an enlightened view of race. "I have always believed it a providential circumstance," he wrote, "that I had that early experience with a negro lad, for it relieved me from that feeling of prejudice which would have hindered me from doing the work for the freedmen," who were placed in his charge years later. I wonder if readers will agree with me that while this sentiment seems entirely laudable at first glance, it somehow leaves a disquieting aftertaste—anyway, we shall see how it stacks up against the facts.

When Otis was nine, his father died of a sudden hemorrhage of his lungs, and Otis was dispatched to live with an aunt and uncle who saw to his schooling. He was a precocious young man, admitted to Bowdoin College at the age of just fifteen. His most notable characteristic, as far as I can tell, was his seriousness of purpose. He determined that he would never take a drink, he declined to inflict on underclassmen the same hazing that he endured as a freshman, and he engaged in no hijinks. He was, in a word, a bit of a stiff, and I think that is what explains the difficulties he encountered in the next chapter of his life, when he gained an appointment to West Point. He was widely disliked at the military academy by, among others, Custis Lee, the son of Robert E. Lee, who was commandant of West Point during Howard's junior and senior years. The precise source of Howard's unpopularity is unclear. He claims to have offended some Southern cadets by his aversion to slavery, though he was not yet an outspoken abolitionist, and he ruffled feathers by defying some of the academy's rules and traditions with which he disagreed, leaving him ostracized and, in his word, feeling "wretched." "I wasn't yet wise enough," he wrote later, "to be silent on the subject of what I regarded as a wrong." This would, I believe, form the crux of the challenge that faced Howard later at the Freedmen's Bureau.

In any case, Howard's social standing at West Point eventually eased, and he graduated fourth in his class, counting among other good friends J. E. B. Stuart, that most Southern of Southern generals. After marrying and fathering a son, Howard was posted to Florida, where the army was trying to push the Seminoles west. By far the most consequential event of this period was Howard's conversion to evangelical Christianity. His younger brother had experienced a calling, and soon Otis Howard did too. "It was the night of the last day of May, 1857, when I had the feeling of sudden relief from the depression that had long been upon me," Howard wrote. "The next morning everything appeared to me to be changed—the sky was brighter, the trees more beautiful, and songs of the birds were never before so sweet to my ears." He wrote his wife, "I was saved through the goodness & mercy of Christ." The "Christian General" had been born again.

Howard next returned to West Point as an instructor in mathematics and then, at the outbreak of the war, resigned his commission and went home to Maine to become colonel of a regiment of a thousand volunteers. In his autobiography, Howard writes with deft irony of the carnival excitement that prevailed as the soldiers boarded their trains on a beautiful spring morning, bade goodbye to their cheering families amid "the swift motion of waving handkerchiefs, flags, and outstretched hands," and headed off to battle having no idea, of course, what awaited them. Howard saw action at the First Battle of Manassas, an ill-fated attempt by the Union in July 1861 to invade northern Virginia that ended in disarray and retreat. While he did not distinguish himself as a commander, Howard stood his ground, demonstrating that he was no coward.

What happened next intrigues me. A few days after the battle, Howard was in his headquarters near Alexandria, Virginia, when a fugitive slave woman presented herself, carrying a two-year-old son, begging for protection and freedom. Moments later a White woman arrived and angrily demanded the return of her property. This was well before the Emancipation Proclamation, and President Lincoln's formal position was that escaped slaves should be returned to their owners—a cruel, untenable "compromise" meant to mollify slave owners in the border states and keep them loyal to the Union. Howard describes himself as "greatly puzzled" with the awful scene that played out before him, but eventually he followed orders and told the owner she could have her slave. When she then demanded a guard, Howard refused. "No, no," he said, "I will not give you a guard. I will never use bayonets to drive a poor girl and her child into bondage." Later that night, the slave woman escaped north to freedom with her son.

I focus on this episode because Howard's conduct was not quite what I expected of the man who later called himself "the Moses of the Negro." Other commanders were more forceful in refusing to remand slaves, notably the flamboyant General John C. Frémont, who unilaterally issued his own premature emancipation proclamation in Missouri. That overreach of authority cost Frémont his job, and I do not say Howard should have done the same, but perhaps he could have been as clever as General Benjamin Butler, who announced that slaves were now "contraband of war" and gave those who escaped refuge in his camps, where they worked to support the Union war effort.

In May 1862, by now promoted to brigadier general, Howard led his men in the Battle of Fair Oaks, Virginia, where he was shot not once but twice in his right arm, which had to be amputated. The courage he demonstrated led Congress to award him the Medal of Honor. He recovered and resumed his military career, which continued to be marred by his shortcomings as a commander. At Chancellorsville, Howard positioned his corps in the wrong direction, and soon afterward at Gettysburg his men were forced to retreat—a pair of embarrassments that earned him the unflattering nickname "Uh-oh Howard."

Fortunately for Howard, he was then reassigned from the Army of the Potomac westward to Tennessee, where he served capably in the battle for Chattanooga and won the confidence of General William Tecumseh Sherman, who praised him for combining "so gracefully and perfectly the polished Christian gentleman and the prompt, zealous, and gallant soldier." Assessing General Howard's military career is beyond the scope of this essay—and the abilities of its author—but I do want to take a crack at explaining how his fortunes improved so dramatically.

Howard himself claimed that experience taught him to be a better general, and this may be so as he demonstrated a newfound skill in the Union's advance through Georgia, including the Battle of Atlanta. Sherman promoted him to command of the Army of the Tennessee, burnishing his reputation. Then, too, some of the earlier criticism of Howard may have resulted from the jealousies that created friction among many Union generals. Serving under a decisive, successful commander like Sherman may have stimulated Howard to act more aggressively.

Perhaps most important, Howard was an ambitious man with friends in high places. As a proud son of Maine, he could count Vice President Hannibal Hamlin in his court and also James G. Blaine, the speaker of the Maine house and later a congressman and speaker of the US House. Howard enjoyed a cordial relationship with President Lincoln, who had certainly learned to be tolerant of flawed generals, and Lincoln foresaw a place for Howard in the work to be done once the war ended.

Howard was in Savannah in January 1865 when Sherman issued his famous Special Field Order No. 15, which gave nearly half a million acres of the sea islands and the Lowcountry of South Carolina, Georgia, and Florida to newly freed slaves. If you have ever wondered where the phrase "forty acres and a mule" comes from, it was Sherman's order, which promised thousands of Black families forty-acre tracts of their own (and later the loan of a government mule to work the land)—a radical redistribution of plantation land abandoned by the owners during the war. The order came at the prodding of Lincoln's secretary of war, Edwin Stanton, who was concerned about the fate of the thousands of emancipated slaves who were following Sherman on his march to the sea.

Stanton and Sherman met in Savannah with a group of twenty Black ministers and had the revolutionary idea of asking them what they wanted. The group's leader, the Reverend Garrison Frazier, a tall, imposing man who had purchased his own freedom, and his wife's, for $1,000 in 1857, gave an eloquent response: "The way we can best take care of ourselves, is to have land, and turn it and till it by our labor." Asked if freed Black people would rather live among White people or by themselves, he said, "I would prefer to live by ourselves, for there is a prejudice against us in the South that will take years to get over." (If you visit Savannah, by the way, you can tour the Green-Meldrim House on Macon Street, where the meeting took place in a high-ceilinged room on the second floor.) Special Order 15 was issued four days later.

Let's take a minute to consider Sherman's order. On the one hand, it was nothing less than a blueprint for rebuilding the entire South, upending a slave economy by granting land ownership to the freed slaves and stripping the planter class of its land as well as its chattels. In the months after the order was issued, Union General Rufus Saxton, an abolitionist, settled some forty thousand freedmen along the coastal lands of South Carolina, where they dutifully toiled away on land they believed was now theirs. In March 1865, after months of bitter debate, Congress finally passed the act creating a Freedmen's Bureau, whose full title—the Bureau of Refugees, Freedmen, and Abandoned Lands—hinted at the revolutionary idea of land redistribution.

But the sturdiness of Sherman's order remained an open question. It was a military order, issued during war, and thus vulnerable to amendment—or reversal—by Congress and the president. And it had fine print: technically, the freedmen would be

RECONSTRUCTION   **117**

renting the land, with an option to buy later on terms that were left deliberately vague.

Sherman was not acting out of a sense of racial enlightenment. During the Battle of Atlanta just a few weeks earlier, he had refused to let Black troops fight for the Union. (The film that now introduces the refurbished cyclorama painting *The Battle of Atlanta* at the Atlanta History Center points out that only one figure among the thousands in the giant painting is Black, and a noncombatant at that.) Sherman's primary motive seems to have been military, to demoralize the enemy. In his memoirs he wrote, "My aim then was, to whip the rebels, to humble their pride, to follow them to their inmost recesses, and make them fear and dread us." He had a paternalistic attitude toward the freedmen and did not believe, as he put it, "that the former slaves would be suddenly, without preparation, manufactured into voters, equal to all others, politically and socially."

President Lincoln, in the months before his death, can fairly be said to have struggled with the challenge of outlining a cohesive, workable plan for Reconstruction. In his so-called last speech, delivered at the White House three days before his assassination, Lincoln grappled with the question of Black suffrage and mused that it might be limited to the "very intelligent" and those who had served in the army—that is, Black voting might be far from universal. He was equally equivocal about giving land to the freedmen.

For all the promise of the Freedmen's Bureau, it is noteworthy that Congress authorized it to exist for only a single year and provided no budget whatsoever. The bureau would be an appendage of the War Department—with the war about to end.

In May 1865, General Howard was summoned to Washington to meet with Stanton, the war secretary, who told him that Lincoln had intended to name him commissioner of the Freedmen's Bureau, adding that the new president, Andrew Johnson, concurred in the choice. Howard accepted readily, a decision his friend Sherman questioned. "I fear you have Hercules' task," Sherman wrote him. "God has limited the power of man, and though in the kindness of your heart you would alleviate all the ills of humanity, it is not in your power to fulfill one tenth part of the expectation of those who formed the Bureau. . . . It is simply impracticable." So it must have seemed when Stanton handed Howard a bushel basket full of reports, correspondence, and other loose papers, and said, "Here, General, here's your bureau!"

By my reckoning, Howard did a good job organizing his infant bureau, operating out of a house in Washington that, in a nice metaphor, had been abandoned by a Southern senator after secession. Missionary groups jumped into the fray, opening schools and providing teachers to bring literacy to the freedmen. The bureau issued tens of thousands of rations to the needy. But on the vital question of giving land to the former slaves, Howard was naive at best and deaf to President Johnson's intentions. Howard sent telegrams to his assistant commissioners in June 1865 asking them to identify the lands in their jurisdictions that were available to be given to freedmen. He did so at the very time that Johnson was signaling sympathy to the defeated Rebels by granting them widespread amnesty and restoring their legal rights, including their property.

At the end of July 1865, Howard began a monthlong vacation back home in Maine. He had earned his furlough, but he chose a bad time to take it. Returning to Washington, Howard met twice with the president and reported with alarm to his wife, "Mr. Johnson is giving up the law pretty fast and I begin to tremble with anxiety for the freedman." Four days later, he wrote her again, saying he feared "the freedmen's rights will not be cared for so much as I could wish." What is striking is the absence of any indication that Howard tried very hard to dissuade the president from the repudiation of land redistribution. In his autobiography, Howard describes making a lukewarm effort to persuade Johnson that White landowners be required to give at least a token homestead of a few acres to their former slaves. "President Johnson was amused," Howard wrote, "and gave no heed to this recommendation." Instead, he ordered Howard explicitly to undo Sherman's orders. "Why did I not resign?" Howard asked. "Because I even yet strongly hoped in some way to befriend the freed people."

Howard may not have fully understood the scope of betrayal at hand, but the freedmen of South Carolina certainly did. On Edisto Island, a group of them had been meeting on a weekly basis to discuss national politics and read the newspapers, and they knew exactly what Howard was going to say to them. When he arrived at a meeting house on Edisto on October 19, 1865, he found some two thousand freedmen filling every seat and jamming the aisles. "Strong evidence of dissatisfaction and sorrow were manifested from every part of the assembly," Howard wrote of the chaotic scene. At length a woman with a sweet voice began singing the spiritual, "Nobody Knows the Trouble I've Seen," and the crowd quieted. Howard explained, in sum, that the freedmen would have to go back to work for their former masters if they wanted to remain on the land they thought they had been given. He asked the freedmen to appoint a committee of three to respond, and what they said—in my view—ranks with Chief Joseph's lament. This is a portion of the letter that the three freedmen wrote to General Howard:

> You ask us to forgive the land owners of our island. *You* only lost your right arm in war and might forgive them. The man who tied me to a tree and gave me 39 lashes and who stripped and flogged my mother and my sister and who will not let me stay in his empty hut except I will do his planting and be satisfied with his price and who combines with others to keep away land from me well knowing I would not have anything to do with him if I had land of my own—that man I cannot well forgive.

Many years later, in his autobiography, Howard concludes his chapter on abandoned lands by noting that President Johnson effected a "complete reversal" of the government's plan to help the emancipated slaves create new lives, leaving his bureau "to make bricks without straw." And then, for reasons I cannot fathom, he added, "After years of thinking and observation, I am inclined to believe that the restoration of their lands to the planters proved for all their future better for the negroes."

I have no idea why Howard wrote that. I think it's fair to argue that giving forty acres of land to the families of all four million freed slaves was not feasible. At the end of the war, by Howard's calculation, the Union controlled enough abandoned land in the South to give each freed slave family only a single acre of land. To give more would have required massive land seizures. The wholesale, forced dispossession of White landowners would have been truly radical, with results that are hard to imagine. It seems entirely possible to me that the reign of terror visited on Black people in the years to come would have stripped them of any lands given them by the Freedmen's Bureau in any case. General Howard could have fought harder and still have lost. And yet. And yet.

I'm drawing my essay to a close at the *beginning* of Reconstruction, without much hope that it could have succeeded—but I think it could have been better than it was. One thing I've learned about slavery in my studies of recent years is that slaves utterly detested being enslaved—an obvious point, perhaps, but as a practical matter it meant that no matter how enlightened and benevolent a slave owner might have been, most of his freed slaves wanted nothing further to do with him, period. Once the chance to give land to the freedmen had been lost, the only real alternative was sharecropping, and that meant freed slaves would have to go back to work for their ex-owners. Indeed, after the promise of forty acres and a mule was withdrawn, the Freedmen's Bureau at Howard's direction began forcing freedmen to sign labor contracts putting them back to work on their old plantations—their worst nightmare.

At its heart, the central dilemma of Reconstruction was almost metaphysical. If the Southern states had no right to secede, as Lincoln argued, then they had never left the Union and were still states, and that meant their citizens—their White citizens—retained legal rights that included keeping their land. If, on the other hand, as the Radical Republicans argued, the Southern states had dissolved themselves, then their citizens had forfeited their rights, including the legal ownership of land, and were subject to the authority of Congress. The argument was rooted mostly in politics. Lincoln's view meant the military and the executive branch—Lincoln himself, as president—would control Reconstruction, while the Radical Republicans' view gave power over Reconstruction to Congress—themselves. The practical result, after Lincoln's death, as Johnson and Congress clashed and veered into impeachment, was the restoration of the status quo ante and the abandonment of land redistribution. As a result, to this day, the net financial worth of Black families in the United States is a fraction of that of White families.

General Howard limped through two more years as head of the Freedmen's Bureau before its doors were closed. He founded Howard University, in Washington, still a beacon of higher learning for Black students. He enjoyed a surprising success in his first assignment in the West, in 1872, with the Apaches, when he persuaded Cochise to make peace and move onto a reservation in Arizona. After his misadventures chasing Chief Joseph, Howard served as superintendent of West Point, wrote his autobiography, and worked tirelessly until his death trying to repair his reputation. There's a wonderful photograph taken in 1904 that shows Howard and Joseph sitting side by side at the commencement ceremony of the Indian Industrial School in Carlisle, Pennsylvania, having at last forgiven each other.

When Howard died, in 1909, I think it's worth noting that "separate but equal" was the law of the land; Jim Crow laws governed the South; the Klan was on the verge of rebirth; race riots were commonplace, including Atlanta's three years earlier; and Woodrow Wilson was waiting in the wings to make things worse.

The historian Eric Foner has called Reconstruction *America's Unfinished Revolution*, as indeed it remains.

TRUMP

When I sat down to begin this chapter on Donald Trump and race, I wasn't at all sure I could find something fresh to say on the subject. But I was wrong. I went back to the story of the Central Park Five and the famous full-page newspaper ad Trump took out in 1989 urging the death penalty for the defendants. The basic details of the case are well known, of course, but I hadn't read the text of the ad in years, and there was an element of it that surprised me.

In the aftermath of the brutal rape and near murder of the jogger, Trisha Meili, there was no lack of fury over an act of savagery that seemed subhuman. At one point, Mayor Ed Koch and Cardinal John J. O'Connor felt moved to caution New Yorkers against giving in to hate and rancor. The ad was Trump's answer. "Mayor Koch has stated that hate and rancor should be removed from our hearts," he wrote. "I do not think so. I want to hate these muggers and murderers. They should be forced to suffer." Emphasizing the point, he added, "Yes, Mayor Koch, I want to hate these murderers and I always will . . . I am looking to punish them . . . I want them to be afraid."

"I want to hate."

By 1989, Trump had begun flirting with the idea of running for president, and he would weigh in from time to time with his views on various issues. His embrace of hate for the Central Park Five was no careless slip of the tongue. He spent $85,000 to run the ad in four daily newspapers in New York City, and to this day—more than three decades later, long after the defendants were exonerated—he has steadfastly refused to apologize or back down an inch. Certainly, we have had hateful politicians in our nation's history—George Wallace comes to mind, and Joe McCarthy—but as far as I can tell, none of them ever explicitly endorsed hatred.

There was another revealing part of the ad. "When I was young," Trump wrote, "I sat in a diner with my father and witnessed two young bullies cursing and threatening a very frightened waitress. Two cops rushed in, lifted up the thugs, and threw them out the door, warning them never to cause trouble again. I miss the feeling of security New York's finest once gave the citizens of this City." Many years later, as president, Trump memorably urged an audience of police officers to play rough with the people they arrest. "When you guys put somebody in the car," he said, "and you're protecting their head, you know, the way you put your hand over? Like, don't hit their head—and they just killed somebody—don't hit their head. I said, you can take the hand away, okay?" Horrified police officials rushed to repudiate what amounted to a casual, lighthearted call for police brutality. As a candidate, Trump urged violent treatment of protesters at his rallies on several occasions, reveling in the persona of a strongman.

Once again, I cannot recall another American politician openly promoting physical violence.

Hate and violence. Fearsome traits in anyone, let alone a president of the United States, but there is a third facet of Trump's personality that makes the mix especially volatile: his penchant for cultivating enemies. Trump's feuds are legendary, from celebrities to journalists to war heroes to professional athletes, and especially his political opponents. His most alarming vendetta was the one he started with Barack Obama by questioning his birthplace. Trump did not invent "birtherism," the theory that Obama was born in Kenya, not Hawaii, but brought the discredited idea roaring back to life in 2011 as President Obama prepared to campaign for reelection. Trump's motive appears to have been twofold, to gain publicity for his own ambition to run for president and to tap in to an ugly vein of prejudice against Obama.

I had forgotten just how disingenuous Trump was in crafting his attack. He gave an interview to ABC's *Good Morning America* in March 2011, in which he bemoaned the criticism leveled at those who brought up the issue, then added, "The reason I have a little doubt, just a little, is because he grew up and nobody knew him." Were he to run, Trump said, "you may go back and interview people from my kindergarten, they'll remember me. Nobody knows who [Obama] is, until later in his life. It's very strange."

In fact, not one but two of Obama's kindergarten teachers had given interviews, in the *Maui Times* in 2009, recalling Obama in great detail, and others remembered him from childhood as well. In April 2011, CNN confronted Trump with the newspaper articles and taped interviews that contradicted him, and he responded with trademark brazenness: "Look, I didn't say that." By then, pleased with the publicity he had garnered reviving the

issue, he grew bolder and began questioning Obama's birth certificate more forcefully. Taking the bait, the media started to press
the president to release a so-called long form birth certificate that
supposedly would resolve the matter once and for all. Alarmed by
polls showing renewed skepticism about his citizenship, Obama
produced the document while muttering darkly about the distrac-
tion of "sideshows and carnival barkers" that manufactured controversy out of thin air.

And then Obama took his revenge. I'm sure most of us
remember the White House Correspondents' Dinner on April
30, 2011, when the president stepped to the microphone, took
aim at Trump, a guest in the audience, and subjected him to withering mockery. The long form certificate had erased doubts about
his place of birth, the president began, eyes twinkling wickedly,
and "no one is happier, no one is prouder, to put this birth certificate matter to rest, than 'The Donald,' and that's because he can
finally get back to focusing on the issues that matter—like, did
we fake the moon landing? What really happened in Roswell?
And where are Biggie and Tupac?" Obama has a born-comedian's
touch and timing, and the audience roared with laughter. Trump
endured the ridicule, a pained smile frozen on his face, and I made
the mistake of thinking the president had slammed the door on
Trump, once and for all.

Looking back, it's easy to see that Trump's humiliation in
front of the national press corps was a pivotal event, one that
deepened his predilection for hating his enemies, and no small
number of pundits have speculated that his candidacy for president was born in that moment. I'm certain he yearned to get even.
But was Trump's attack on Obama an act of racism? Is Trump a
racist? The answer is entirely subjective, of course, but I mean to

explore the question because Trump's presidency affected race in America in a thousand different ways, some of them consequential and enduring, and I believe it will help if we can understand what he was up to.

Obviously, no one has ever mistaken Trump for a warm-hearted liberal on matters of race, but I have wondered over the years whether his animus was genuine or more a matter of pure calculation, meant to secure his place—as it did—with White voters harboring grievances or worse feelings toward people of color. Perhaps it does not matter, but I recall having an insight into Trump's thinking when the late congressman John Lewis boycotted his inaugural in 2017, saying Trump was not a "legitimate" president. Trump's counterattack was revealing. Lewis, he said in a tweet, "should spend more time on fixing and helping his district, which is in horrible shape and falling apart (not to mention crime infested) rather than falsely complaining about the election results." As a longtime resident of Georgia's Fifth Congressional District, I shook my head at the description. While it certainly has poor neighborhoods, the Fifth also contains the world's busiest airport, the CNN Center, Georgia Tech, Emory University, the Centers for Disease Control, Centennial Olympic Park, the headquarters of the Coca-Cola Company, and Buckhead (the White, wealthy residential section so memorably lampooned for its lush, bosomy lawns by Tom Wolfe in *A Man in Full*). Suggesting it was a slum struck me as strange and ignorant.

Two years later, Trump got into a dustup with another Black congressman, the late Elijah Cummings, and reprised his earlier brand of attack, calling Cummings's Baltimore district "disgusting, rat and rodent infested." He added, "No human being would want to live there." I came to the conclusion that Trump actually believes that almost all African Americans are poor and live in wretched, dangerous neighborhoods. His frequent challenge to Black voters—"What the hell have you got to lose?"—reflects the same Dickensian view. In a White House meeting with congressional leaders in 2018, Trump memorably complained about accepting immigrants from Haiti and "shithole countries" in Africa and the Americas rather than nations such as Norway. In a word: he's a bigot.

Trump came of age as the son of a New York developer, Fred Trump, who refused to rent apartments to Black people, instructing his agents to mark their applications with a *C* for colored. In 1973, the Justice Department sued Trump Management for housing discrimination and Donald Trump made his debut on the front page of the *New York Times*, flatly denying the allegations. By one account, though, he said to a government lawyer during an unguarded moment, "You know, you don't want to live with them either."

A half century later, I don't believe Trump's thinking on race has changed a bit. Campaigning for reelection in 2020, literally without a platform and unable to articulate proposals for a second term, he ran on a promise to keep "low-income housing" out of the suburbs—his intended subtext being that he meant to keep Black people from moving into White neighborhoods, the exact tactic he had followed with his father.

Reflecting on Trump and race, I was struck by the idea of place. Trump seems to believe that Black people have a place and should remain in it. In an appearance before Congress in 2019, Trump's defrocked lawyer, Michael Cohen, testified, "While we were once driving through a struggling neighborhood in Chicago, he commented that only black people could live that way."

Feuding with a bloc of four progressive congresswomen of color, he asked, "Why don't they go back and help the totally broken and crime-infested places from which they came?"

Seen through this lens, Trump's brand of racism comes into closer focus. The Central Park Five did not belong in the park. Protesters did not belong at his rallies. Obama did not belong in the White House. The common thread is the "other" invading turf that does not belong to them. Perhaps the most dramatic illustration of Trump's territoriality was the decision in June 2020 to have lawful protesters cleared by force from Lafayette Square so that he could walk from the White House to St. John's Episcopal Church for a photo opportunity clutching a Bible. "What ensued," the *New York Times* reported, "was a burst of violence unlike any seen in the shadow of the White House in generations." The protesters were exercising their constitutional right to assemble, but to Trump they were interlopers on his doorstep, to be swept away by martial force. On an opéra bouffe level, Trump's instinct for primacy of place was illustrated perfectly at a NATO meeting in 2017 when he rudely shoved the prime minister of Montenegro out of his way and seized the front and center spot for a group photo of world leaders.

Trying to guess when Trump is speaking honestly is a risky undertaking, I know, but there was a revealing moment for me in September 2020, during the campaign, when Bob Woodward released a tape recording of one of his interviews with Trump for the book *Rage*. With awkward earnestness, Woodward laid out a definition of White privilege and asked Trump whether it "has isolated and put you in a cave . . . as it put me . . . and that we have to work our way out of it to understand the anger and the pain black people feel in this country? Do you see?" Trump sounded genuinely surprised "No!" he answered. "You, you really drank the Kool-Aid, didn't you? Just listen to you! Wow. No, I don't feel that at all." I think the concept of White privilege was genuinely alien to him.

How damaging was it to have a man of Trump's sensibilities serve as president for four years? How perilous will it be having him lurk offstage as ex-president, reaching out to his loyal base and running again? It's hard to say. As I reflect on the dangerous character traits I see in Trump—the hatred, violence, and feuding—I confess to being surprised that the consequences were not even worse. Certainly, he gave aid and comfort to White supremacists. The FBI reported the highest number of hate crimes in a decade in 2019—but the record year for such crimes was 2008, the year we elected America's first Black president, so it was not as if Trump invented racial discord out of thin air. Those who see him as a symptom of racial division, rather than a cause, may have a point.

Just as electing Obama failed to usher in a post-racial era, electing Trump may not have significantly worsened race relations that were on shaky ground to begin with. Indeed, thanks to matters beyond Trump's control, his term ended with more White Americans than ever before telling pollsters they recognize the enduring discrimination that confronts African Americans. The one truly frightening decision Trump might have made, to invoke the Insurrection Act and send active military into US cities to quell unrest in the spring of 2020, was shelved after his defense secretary, Mark Esper, publicly opposed it.

Trump's frequent claim that he had done more for African Americans—or, as he sometimes said, "the blacks"—than any president since Abraham Lincoln was the sort of shameless hyperbole that tickled his supporters and left others either shaking their heads or gnashing their teeth. His legislative record, which included the First Step Act, a significant reform of prison sentencing, was otherwise threadbare, according to most Black leaders.

So a nagging mystery for me in the aftermath of the 2020 election was how Trump managed to win the support of some 12 percent of Black voters, an increase from his showing in 2016. Writing in the *Atlantic*, John McWhorter suggested an answer. Racism is a fact of life to many African Americans, he argued, and for them, "Trump's policies, or even just some of them, or even just the cut of his jib, may seem more important than what Trump would say about them in private—or public." McWhorter's point was a close cousin of the excuse many White voters gave for supporting Trump, that his politics and policies overrode his character flaws.

Yet as president, Trump was not just the head of government, he was also the head of state, the personification of our country. Excusing open bigotry in the leader of the United States of America is utterly dismaying and, I fear, damaging in ways that may not yet be fully grasped. Perhaps Trump's brand of racism was not as corrosive as, say, Woodrow Wilson's, whose lofty airs and ideals and progressive politics masked a truly stark view of African Americans as inferior. Trump had such ugly things to say about so many of his fellow human beings—women, "foreigners," cabinet members who failed to do his bidding—that his racism seemed part and parcel of general misanthropy. It's hard to imagine any parent holding him up to a child as a role model. Still, if I've learned anything in a half century studying racism, it's that no excuse for it is acceptable and no explanation is benign.

Trump's enduring support among evangelical Christians, for instance, has been explained away as a matter of policy over character, but there may be another, more insidious explanation. In *White Too Long*, theologian and sociologist Robert Jones cites survey results showing that White Christians harbor a host of bigoted attitudes toward African Americans, even as they profess positive emotions for them. "White Christians," Jones writes, "think of themselves as people who hold warm feelings toward African Americans while simultaneously embracing a host of racist and racially resentful attitudes that are inconsistent with that assertion." In a sense, they resemble Trump himself, who denies having a racist bone in his body while doing and saying things that are plainly racist. Among the questions Jones asked White Christians was whether they viewed Confederate monuments as expressions of Southern pride or as symbols of racism; they tilted heavily toward Trump's view that the monuments represent heritage. And they gave outsize support to phrases such as "if blacks would only try harder, they could be just as well off as whites" and "today discrimination against whites has become as big a problem as discrimination toward blacks and other minorities."

If we learned anything about race from Trump's presidency, it seems to me, it was the crucial need for empathy. If White Americans hope to arrive at a more enlightened understanding of the burdens that weigh on Black Americans, we have many miles to walk in others' shoes. I can't think of anyone in public life who has ever suffered a more obvious lack of empathy than Donald Trump, and that sad fact sums up his legacy on race. He chose to hate.

COLORBLIND

One evening at my twentieth prep-school reunion, a classmate banged on a glass and interrupted dinner to solicit our help for a magazine article he was writing. He proceeded to pass out a questionnaire designed to show that we had abandoned most of the ideals we held when we graduated, in 1966, and were now morphing into hypocritical Babbitts as we crept toward middle age. It was an exercise that broke down quickly amid jeers and catcalls, like a scene from *Animal House*, as we objected to serving as guinea pigs in a test rigged against us. The question that stuck in my mind was, "Would you let your daughter marry Kareem Abdul-Jabbar?"

I'm pretty sure the first thought most of us had was, *Oh, for heaven's sake! That old chestnut!* Would you let your daughter marry a Black man? The question was a staple of my childhood in the Eisenhower '50s, as White liberals contrived to show that expressions of racial goodwill in the abstract would not survive the specter of a Black suitor asking for the hand of a fair daughter. I can remember friends of my parents taking the bait, arguing that they were fine with interracial marriage but worried about the burdens that *others* might impose on the imaginary couple. Right. Sure. The simple truth was that White supremacy was so deeply ingrained in the United States in 1954, when *Brown v. Board of Education* began to shake the walls, that most White people did indeed harbor prejudices. But I believe those who tried to overcome them, however imperfectly, deserve a lot more credit than those who fought Black individuals' advancement tooth and nail.

From my perch at the keyboard today, those conversations of the '50s and '60s, even the '80s, seem almost prehistoric. In my author's note, I mentioned Eleanor Roosevelt's appearance on the cover of *Ebony* in 1953 with the headline "Some of My Best Friends Are Negroes." How we got from that point to where we are now is a question I've been studying for a half century, throughout my career and into retirement, with little confidence that I have the right answers but with the conviction that we have made progress even if it seems at times that we have not.

By 1986, I'd been working at the *Atlanta Journal-Constitution* for a decade and a half. In many respects, I was a seasoned observer of racial politics. One offshoot of the Atlanta Child Murders was the creation of a talk show on WSB-TV, the city's dominant local news operation, hosted by Ron Sailor, a Black reporter (and preacher) who had earned widespread respect for his coverage of the cases. I signed on as one of the founding panelists on the show, called *Sunday News Conference*, when it debuted in May 1982. We aired on Sundays at 6:30 p.m., just after the local news, a coveted time slot that no public affairs show could command today. We enjoyed good ratings, and thanks to Sailor we had quite a following in the Black community. I was stopped occasionally by Black viewers, who would call out greetings such as, "You're the TV dude!" I found the sense of familiarity valuable during city elections, when I was welcomed into all manner of venues in Black neighborhoods.

But looking back, I realize I was still grappling with many of the underlying tensions and unresolved issues of race relations beyond the ballot box. Our newsroom was diversifying, and I enjoyed discussing and debating matters of race with my Black colleagues. I am embarrassed to recall believing back then that Black folks needed to assimilate into the dominant culture—needed, I argued, to give their children conventional names, like George and Martha, not Quemishia and Jamarcus—if they hoped to succeed. I was mistaken, of course, as any number of Black figures, from Mahalia Jackson and Althea Gibson to Thurgood Marshall and Muhammad Ali, had already demonstrated quite plainly and as Oprah Winfrey was in the process of giving an exclamation point. Soon Condoleezza Rice would be secretary of state and, more impressive still, a member of Augusta National.

My thinking was rooted in the honorable old notion of a "colorblind" society, an ideal I am willing to concede was naive—but not before sharing a story. Ray Jenkins was a White newspaperman from the Deep South who enjoyed a distinguished career on the enlightened side of the racial divide. He was the roommate of my boss at the *Journal-Constitution*, Jim Minter, at the University of Georgia, and it was Minter who told me about him. Jenkins was just twenty-nine years old in 1959 when he became city editor of the *Alabama Journal*, the afternoon newspaper in Montgomery, where he would drop in occasionally at the Dexter Avenue Baptist Church to interview its pastor, Martin Luther King Jr. On one visit, Jenkins mentioned having ancestors who had been slave owners in northern Georgia. "And yet," he recalled King answering, "you and I can hold this respectful talk—you, the son of slave owners, and I, the son of slaves who once lived together in the Red Hills of Georgia. Isn't that reassuring?" As they parted, King asked if he could do anything for Jenkins, who replied that he would be honored if King included the thought in a speech one day. Four years later, Jenkins was listening on the radio when King gave his "I Have a Dream" speech at the March on Washington, intoning in a rolling cadence, "I have a dream that one day on the Red Hills of Georgia, the sons of former slaves and the sons of former slave owners will be able to sit down together at the table of brotherhood." Jenkins, who died at the age of eighty-nine in October 2019, considered that moment the high point of his career, greater than his Pulitzer Prize.

If King could dream that his four children "will one day live in a nation where they will not be judged by the color of their skin but by the content of their character," then perhaps we should not be too quick to dismiss a colorblind society as an unrealistic, unreachable goal. The roadblocks to achieving it are not hard to enumerate, and I do not mean to write a textbook listing them, but I would like to explore one thread of history that may explain in a fresh light why we have faltered along our way.

When the time finally came to end segregation as the law of the land, it arrived in the form of the US Supreme Court's unanimous decision in *Brown v. Board of Education*, in 1954, holding that "separate but equal" was inherently unequal and thus unconstitutional. What made the case so compelling, of course, was that the victims were innocent children. No one with a heart could remain unmoved by the plight of Black children trapped in wretched schools, their lives stunted before they had really begun. Who could avoid a shiver of shame at those studies with dolls that revealed self-loathing in Black children who had been poisoned by the racism of the society that surrounded them? In researching my book *Atlanta Rising*, I recall learning that Georgia adopted its first statewide sales tax in 1951 in large part to raise money for a last-ditch effort to improve Black schools and raise them to a semblance of equality, in hopes of fending off the looming court decision. The governor at the time, Herman Talmadge, once calculated that he spent more on education than all of the governors of Georgia before him, *combined*—and still made barely a dent in the disparity of Black schools and White schools.

My argument—and it is a dangerous one—is that the very thing that made *Brown* so pivotal, the well-being of children, sowed its fate as a toxically divisive issue because it ignited fear in White parents that *their* children might have to pay the price for rectifying the situation by going to school with Black children. Do not mistake me. There was racism coursing through the veins of this fear, but my point is that parents, however misguided, will go to extremes if they think they must to protect their children. White parents thought their children would be harmed by having Black children as schoolmates and acted accordingly. My point is not that America's public schools should have remained segregated, obviously, but rather that tearing down the walls might better have started elsewhere.

I stumbled onto this thought in the 1990s when I was researching *Secret Formula* and *Atlanta Rising*, reading the private papers of the business leaders and politicians who shepherded Atlanta during the civil rights era and adopted positions on race considered progressive for their time. In particular, Robert Woodruff, who ran the Coca-Cola Company and had immense influence on the city's mayors of the day, recognized that if he wanted to sell his soft drink to people of color in the United States and around the world, he could not have his hometown associated with the sort of violent resistance—fire hoses, tear gas, and German shepherds—that ruined the reputations of Birmingham and other Southern cities. And so Atlanta abided by court orders and deseg-regated its parks and buses when ordered to do so. What struck me, though, was the genuine difficulty Woodruff and his fellow business leaders had in the 1960s coming to grips with the public accommodations section of the Civil Rights Act and its insistence that the owners of private enterprises—restaurants, hotels, stores, theaters—could not discriminate on the basis of race.

These men were fierce capitalists, I came to understand, and it went deep against the grain with them to suggest that a private business owner could be forced by the government to serve a cus-tomer he did not wish to serve, for whatever reason. In February 1964, when the US House of Representatives took up the Civil Rights Act, the liberal, racially enlightened congressman from Atlanta, Charles Weltner, voted against the bill because of the public accommodations provision, explaining that while prejudice was morally wrong, "I am loath to impose by nationwide legis-lation that moral judgment on others in areas clearly within the sphere of individual action." By autumn, when the bill returned from the Senate, Weltner had changed his mind and became the lone member of Congress from the South to vote in favor of it. But his earlier vote represented the thinking of a great many White Southerners otherwise inclined to give ground on segregation.

As it happened, though, the swiftest, smoothest success of the civil rights era was the widespread acceptance of integration in private businesses that served the public. There are bigots, I con-cede, who even today do not wish to sit next to people of color at a movie theater or on an airplane, but their numbers are small. The vast majority of White Americans are perfectly comfortable shopping, dining, staying in hotels, and otherwise mixing with Black people. And the reason, I think, is that Black and White people alike share pretty much the same experience of being out in public. Buying clothes in a department store does not trigger discomfort over some fundamental difference in the ways Black and White people go shopping. I am not suggesting we've achieved some kind of utopia. Black people are routinely shadowed in stores, profiled as potential shoplifters. Clerks occasionally refuse to let Black shoppers try on clothes in changing rooms. Black and White customers still have brushes rooted in prejudice, some of them horrific, but they have grown relatively rare. A CBS poll conducted in 2014 found that 83 percent of White and 84 percent of Black respondents believed the Civil Rights Act had improved the lives of African Americans. Adults engaged in communal activities, such as working side by side in factories and offices or serving in the armed forces, have achieved the greatest success in becoming colorblind. Familiarity has bred tolerance.

School desegregation, meanwhile, has failed on an epic scale, and the mere mention of busing or other remedies can ignite fierce, even violent political opposition to this day. Had I a magic wand, would I go back in time and postpone *Brown*? Flip a switch so that the Civil Rights Act and Voting Rights Act came first, and *Brown* later? No, I suppose not. Who can guess what resultant mischief doing so might release, playing what-if with the most intractable social problem our nation has ever known? Would White adults who had become comfortable interacting with Black adults behave differently as parents worried about the education of their children? Perhaps not. But perhaps so. Even in modest numbers, that might have led to greater success in integrating our public schools.

I mean only to provoke some thinking about the reasons that progress on race has been so glacial, so fraught with backward steps. When, after several years of foot-dragging, the Atlanta Public Schools system finally implemented a plan of desegregation in 1961, its leaders handpicked nine Black children of sterling character to attend four of the city's high schools. Their attendance went off without a hitch, a textbook case of gradualism at work—the notion that if you moved slowly, built confidence, and curtailed fears, you would at least be headed in the right direction. But gradualism defies the laws of political physics. Once begun, change accelerates. Within a decade, the Atlanta schools were 80 percent Black as White people fled. Dr. King begat leaders who demanded more change, faster, by any means necessary. Do I blame Black people for insisting on the equality they won in the Civil War and that was denied to them for a century and then withheld in the face of Supreme Court decisions and acts of Congress? No. Of course not. I do not mean to blame the victims. I am just saying it might have been done differently, with better results.

The fundamental shortcoming of colorblindness, I came to realize, was that it asked Black people to become White. As the emergence of the "Black Is Beautiful" movement in the 1960s demonstrated, being Black was not just a matter of skin color but of culture. Asking Black Americans to assimilate like the immigrant waves of Irish or Italians not only ignored the debilitating legacy of slavery, it asked African Americans to renounce the contributions they had made to our communal culture. In a sense, my small campaign to persuade Black colleagues to abandon fanciful first names for their children was akin to asking them to give up jazz or gospel. "I am not a ward of America," James Baldwin once wrote. "I am not an object of missionary charity. I am one of the people who built the country." Or as Frederick Douglass put it, speaking of the role of Black people in American history, "We came when it was a wilderness. . . . *We* leveled your forests; *our hands* removed the stumps from the field. . . . We have been with you . . . in adversity, and by the help of God will be with you in prosperity." Amen to that.

Strictly as a matter of skin color, Black Americans have been assimilated for centuries. Four fifths of American slaves were born in this country, not captured in Africa and brought here. Their gene pool is shared with White Americans. According to the *New York Times*, the vast majority of Black Americans have White ancestry—usually male, by the way. Back in the '50s, when White fathers rejected the notion of their daughters marrying Black men, one Black observer remarked with razor sharpness, "You mean Negroes are not going to be marrying your *wife's* daughters. We've been marrying *your* daughters for a long time."

Bit by bit, day by day, generation by generation, we are becoming not a color-*blind* society but a color-*blend* society, as racial intermarriage produces children who grow up to win Academy Awards, the Masters, and, yes, the presidency. I will get to the bad stuff in a later chapter—and it truly is bad stuff—but I mean to end here on a hopeful note. In 1896, when the US Supreme Court made segregation the law of the land, embracing the notion of "separate but equal" in its *Plessy v. Ferguson* decision, the loser of the case was Homer A. Plessy. A resident of New Orleans, he had boarded a train in defiance of Louisiana's Separate Car Act and appealed his conviction up the line. Plessy was one-eighth

Black, an "octoroon" in the parlance of the day, and that was more than enough to make him a Black man in the eyes of the law. Today, I honestly believe, his is the emerging face of America.

By the way, the lone dissenter in the decision, Justice John Marshall Harlan, protested that the Constitution "is color-blind" and must not tolerate discrimination based on race. I give him the final word.

REBECCA LOGAN

Rebecca Logan came into my life when I was three or four years old. She was our part-time cook and housekeeper. She was the first Black person I'd ever known. And while I have met, liked, respected, admired, and even revered quite a number of Black people in the decades since then, she remains the only Black person I have ever loved. I'm pretty sure she's the only Black person who has ever loved me.

White people writing about "the help" is a dangerous undertaking, I know. Yet my debt to Rebecca is so great that I have no choice. She taught me my first lessons about race, and they remain the most enduring. If we are ever to reconcile race in this country, it is going to flow from a recognition that Black people and White people come to the table from such fundamentally different and uneven places that they meet as strangers, yet over and over again they manage to find the common humanity in one another and build on it. But before I get too carried away with my sermon, let me introduce you to Rebecca. You're going to like her.

She stood five feet two and was solid as a ham. Her coloring was mahogany. When she came to work for us in 1952, she was in her early thirties, divorced, the mother of two—a son, Donnie, and a daughter, Helene. She lived in Mount Vernon, New York, not far from our home in Bronxville. Rebecca was not solely a domestic. At one time she worked as a switchboard operator at Grasslands, the large public hospital in Westchester County. One of her gifts was a lovely speaking voice and the ability to sound "White" when she chose to. That's how she got hired at Grasslands.

But she could talk "Black" too, when circumstances warranted, as they did one spring day when she brought Helene to our house and put the two of us in a double stroller for a walk in the park along the Bronx River. I was not just a White boy, mind you, I was towheaded and blue-eyed, a tiny Aryan. Helene, a few years older, was her mother's color. A White man passed by us and stopped to admire the two of us in the stroller. And then, being a wise guy, he said to Rebecca, "What lovely children! Are they both yours?" She eyed him evenly for a moment and replied sweetly, "Dass right. But dey had different daddies!" He was not amused. But my mother certainly was when told about it later.

Rebecca did not brook any expression of racial prejudice. I recall an elementary school classmate coming to our house after school one day and pulling out a miniature Aunt Jemima doll from his pocket when he thought she wasn't looking. But she was always looking. She snatched it out of his hand and gave him as thorough a talking-to about race and respect as I've ever heard. Like all of us, she could be tin-eared: In our very early days, she explained to me that her Black skin was "safe" and would not rub off on me. Even at that early age, I felt insulted that she thought I might think so. It is a small irony, I suppose, that the only part of Rebecca I actually learned to fear was white—her palm, which administered the occasional spanking I earned. The rest of her, the brown rest of her, was warm and comforting.

The molten lava of race in America in the 1950s erupted only occasionally in our household, but when it did, we all suffered terrible burns. It became a tradition that Rebecca would come to our house on Thanksgiving and Christmas to cook our holiday meals, and like most White families of our time and place we did not overly concern ourselves that this might be keeping her from her own children. One Thanksgiving, Rebecca arrived with her daughter in tow and announced to my mother that Helene would be joining us at the table for dinner. With her heart knocking, my mother replied firmly that Helene would be eating in the kitchen with Rebecca. We did not speak of it again, but I am certain none of us ever got over it. In later years, I realized that my mother, a kind woman, was not merely enforcing a harsh racial code but was also sparing Helene from a lonely and awkward meal with three White strangers.

Despite my efforts to impart a literary touch to this chapter, it would be just another sappy memoir of a privileged White boy with deep affection for his nanny, except that my family's fortunes took an awful turn and thrust Rebecca into a pivotal role in my life. When I was eleven, my father succumbed to the mental illness that had been incubating in him for years. The formal diagnosis was paranoid schizophrenia, though I recall my mother telling me that one of the many psychiatrists who examined him told her with weary directness, "Mrs. Allen, we can call it whatever we want, but he's just plain crazy." Among other things, he thought my mother was trying to kill him. One morning, in a grim cliché, men in white coats arrived in a padded wagon and took him away.

My father's illness hit my mother like a wrecking ball, affecting her own health. In the coming years she suffered terribly from rheumatoid arthritis, which we believed was triggered by the trauma. She, too, was occasionally hospitalized. My mother's mother came to live with us for a while, but in many ways the anchor of our family became Rebecca. The kindnesses she lavished on me were endless. But the moment that still matters most to me is a small one. When I was about twelve, I was scheduled to attend a cotillion of some sort that required a coat and tie. Both my parents were absent, and Rebecca was staying at the house to look after me. It did not occur to me that she would know how to tie a necktie, and I went to her in some agitation saying we would have to find someone to assist me. What I remember so vividly was the look she gave me, a combination of gentle amusement and genuine exasperation, as she asked me why in the world I would assume that she did not know how to tie a necktie. She proceeded to do so, quite deftly. I had hurt her feelings, though I believe she was assuaged by the satisfaction she took in proving me mistaken.

Most White people, no matter how well intentioned, have moments in their lives when they make an assumption about a Black person that is rooted in prejudice. The classic example would be handing your car keys to a Black man standing outside a restaurant, assuming he's the valet, when in fact he's a fellow patron. These microaggressions, as they've come to be called, are innocent enough, I think, from a White perspective, but I can only imagine the cumulative effect they have on the Black people who encounter and suffer them. Any negative assumption about a person based on skin color is a bad thing. Not a sin, not necessarily hatred—but a small, ignorant cruelty that we owe it to one another to avoid. Because of Rebecca, I learned to try to curtail mine.

My reliance on Rebecca ebbed as I went off to boarding school and then college, but she continued to help my mother, and she remained a fixture at the holidays. For a time, we shared Thanksgiving and Christmas with another family, and Rebecca established a modus operandi by standing in the open kitchen door to converse with us during the meals. Such were the strained conventions of the time. After I moved to Atlanta, I continued to return home for Thanksgiving and Christmas, and by then I simply sat in the kitchen with Rebecca while she cooked so we could visit. When I brought my wife-to-be, Linda, home for the first time, Rebecca betrayed one of her own prejudices, announcing in advance that she was not going to accept a Southerner as my fiancée. When Linda arrived, she wrapped Rebecca in a bear hug, told her what a fine job she had done raising me, and that was that.

My job as a reporter and political columnist with the *Atlanta Constitution* brought me into close contact, and often friendship, with a host of prominent Black leaders—Julian Bond, John Lewis, Andrew Young, Maynard Jackson—and Rebecca genuinely enjoyed having me tell her about them. One of her favorite stories was the time I met Bennie Ivey, a fixture of the civil rights movement in Atlanta: we chatted for a few minutes at a political rally, and when we parted, she turned to a friend and said, "Lord! That is the whitest white man I have ever seen!" During my short stint at CNN, Rebecca and her daughter, Helene, came to Atlanta, and I had the pleasure of taking them out to lunch and showing them around the studios. She was impressed that I had covered Jesse Jackson's campaign for the presidency. I know she was proud of me because she took to calling me her third child.

Later still, age robbed Rebecca of her mobility and then her vision. I hadn't realized how profoundly religious she was until our conversations in those later years. One of the best gifts I have ever thought to give was an audiobook of James Earl Jones reading the Bible that I sent to Rebecca so that she could continue to hear the Word after she could no longer read it. We talked from time to time for another twenty years. She had the habit many Black women share of signing off by saying, "Have a blessed day." She lived well into her nineties, long after I had lost both my parents, and I mourn her still.

When I sat down to craft this chapter, I thought of "Grady's Gift," the remarkable story that Howell Raines wrote in the *New York Times* Sunday magazine in 1991. Howell and I were colleagues at the *Constitution* in the 1970s, before he moved on to the *Times* and became its executive editor. He was always a very felicitous writer, and "Grady's Gift" won a Pulitzer Prize. It told the story of his relationship with his family's maid, Grady, as Raines grew up in Birmingham, Alabama, in the 1950s. In one of its finest passages, he wrote, "There is no trickier subject for a writer from the South than that of the affection between a black person and a white one in the unequal world of segregation. For the dishonesty upon which such a society is founded makes every emotion suspect, makes it impossible to know whether what flowed between two people was honest feeling or pity or pragmatism."

Well, trust me, it's no easy feat for a writer from the North either. But I would be doing a grave disservice to Rebecca if I have failed to convey my certainty that I knew her well enough to know her heart and to know that heart loved me. An awful unfairness dictated Rebecca's place in the world, but she was a free woman at heart, and she made certain I knew it.

TV

In the 1990s, Atlanta was confronted with questions about how to deal with a phenomenon called "Freaknik," the annual spring gathering of students from historically Black colleges and universities. Because of its location, Black political leadership, and reputation for embracing civil rights, Atlanta became a magnet for Freaknik, culminating in 1994 when an estimated two hundred thousand visitors converged on the city, cruising the streets in cars and creating a traffic nightmare. For those not trapped in the gridlock, Freaknik had a certain comic aspect. In his 1998 novel *A Man in Full*, Tom Wolfe mocked the White burghers of Atlanta, some of them looking on aghast from the grounds of the exclusive Piedmont Driving Club, for "freaking out" as the Black students gave them "a snootful of the future."

I, too, was amused at the time by what I considered to be an overreaction to the event. On our local talk TV show, by now renamed *The Georgia Gang*, we took up the topic during the run-up to Freaknik one year, and I commented that I thought there was going to be a heavy turnout "because I was just downtown, and I

saw a Volvo with the ethnic trim package." The taping was interrupted by a loud guffaw from my cameraman, an ordinarily tac-
iturn Black man, who found the image of pencil-thin tires and
rotating silvery wheels on a staid Swedish Volvo to be hilarious.

Then the footage from the streets began to flow into our
newsroom and others, and soon the worm turned. The treatment
of many of the women in Freaknik was shocking. They were
groped, or worse, and treated with utter disrespect, most of it
uninvited and deeply offensive. Over time, it was not just uptight
White people who reacted but Black adults who saw the pictures
and decided that Freaknik needed to come to a halt. One of the
city's prominent anchorwomen, Monica Kaufman, memorably
denounced the behavior she witnessed, on air. My old colleague at
the *Journal-Constitution*, Cynthia Tucker, the editorial page editor, wrote, "The most disturbing characteristic of Freaknik is the
unvarnished misogyny exhibited by so many of the young men.
They assault women, surrounding them in packs, groping them,
tearing off their clothes. Inevitably, there are reports of rape."
Many factors contributed to the end of Freaknik, notably a police
crackdown on traffic violations, including impounding dozens
of cars, but it was leaders in the Black community who closed
the door on Freaknik, sparing the city any second-guessing that
White racism had been the cause.

Purely by coincidence, I began this chapter in the late spring
of 2020, just as the nation was horrified by the police killing of
George Floyd in Minneapolis and then convulsed by the protests
that erupted in scores of cities in response. I had been planning
to reflect on the influence of television and video cameras on race
relations, and here came the exclamation point before I had written a word. The trial of the police officer who killed George Floyd

was televised, and his conviction on a charge of murder illustrated an advance in justice for all to see. That TV news coverage and cameras have had a profound impact on attitudes about race is not an original insight, obviously, but as I poked into the subject I was struck by how much deeper and more pervasive the influence has been than I first thought.

I started with a simple timeline. One crucial turning point for race in America was the return of Black veterans from World War II. Having fought fascism abroad, they had little patience for repression at home. Windows in Black households bore the famous double V, for victory over fascism at home and abroad. The return of Black GIs coincided roughly with the rise of television and its transformative ability to show viewers, not just tell them, what was happening. I think TV had a subtle effect at first—showing Jackie Robinson and other Black players leading the Brooklyn Dodgers to a series of pennants in the 1950s, say, or letting White viewers see how dignified Rosa Parks was, or how ugly the scene turned in 1957 at Central High in Little Rock, Arkansas, when Governor Orval Faubus defied a court order to desegregate the school and President Eisenhower sent in federal troops to enforce the law.

But it was violence, of course, that galvanized the American public and led directly to some of the most pivotal changes involving race. The fire hoses and police dogs that Bull Connor turned loose on Black children in Birmingham in 1963 left a searing, indelible afterimage on the nation's collective retina and prompted passage of the long-stalled Civil Rights Act the next year. The horrors of "Bloody Sunday" on the Edmund Pettus Bridge in Selma, Alabama, in 1965 drove passage of the Voting Rights Act. In 1968, rioting in American cities after the assassination of Martin Luther King Jr. fed a backlash that badly damaged the cause of civil rights and led to the election of Richard Nixon on a platform of law and order.

And then, in a sense, we changed the channel. Network news turned its focus to political protests against the war in Vietnam. The national debate over race became more abstract. The courts took up affirmative action, leading to the *Bakke* decision in 1978 from a Supreme Court that did not allow cameras in its chambers. A gentler effect was underway on television, in its programming rather than its news. The show *Julia*, starring Diahann Carroll as a nurse, not a servant, debuted in 1968 and paved the way for the upwardly mobile Jeffersons and their "dee-luxe apartment in the sky" in the 1970s. Later yet came *The Cosby Show*, the highest rated program on TV for five consecutive seasons in the 1980s, depicting an upper-middle-class Black family. My belief in a colorblind society did not seem so far-fetched when I watched those shows.

If you were White, it was possible to believe that great strides in race relations had taken place. To be sure, there was a "Southern strategy" in place in our politics, turning a once Solid South from Democratic to Republican, rooted entirely in lingering prejudice and resistance to integration. But it is instructive, I think, that loose talk of "welfare queens" and "states' rights" and the like were called dog whistles because they could only be heard, not seen. A fair number of White people, citing civil rights legislation and the spending of millions of dollars on the War on Poverty, effectively washed their hands of the matter and decided it was time to let Black folks lift themselves up by their own bootstraps.

An awakening came in 1991 when the police beating of Rodney King in Los Angeles was captured on a bystander's video camera and then shown on a local TV newscast. The sight of

an apparently hobbled and passive Black man being struck violently with batons by police officers more than fifty times was
gut-wrenching. It is a commonplace of TV news today for anchors
to warn viewers that they might find upcoming footage "disturbing." Well, the footage of King truly was disturbing. It seemed an
open-and-shut case of gross police brutality. Four officers were
fired, charged with assault and the use of excessive force, and most
people assumed they would be convicted. But a change of venue
moved the trial to a conservative White community, Simi Valley,
and on April 29, 1992, a mostly White jury acquitted three of the
defendants and hung up on the fourth. Rioting erupted in Los
Angeles and lasted six days, costing sixty-three lives and nearly
$1 billion in property damage.

I was working at CNN at the time. I was inside headquarters
in Atlanta the day after the verdict when rioting broke out in the
city and reached the sidewalks outside our building. A mob of
young Black men set upon a White pedestrian, Fred Schuttenberg, and beat him nearly to death. Had I left work early that
day, the body on the sidewalk could very easily have been mine,
a realization that sat like a cold rock in the pit of my stomach.
The rioting in Los Angeles, Atlanta, and many other cities, was
shown on television, of course, and the scenes of violence exposed
a deep gulf of perception between Black people and White people.
Abusive treatment at the hands of police, a fact of life for many
Black people, was little known or recognized by most Whites. It
would take many years—and many videos—for White Americans to appreciate the frustration and rage of Black Americans at
the unfair treatment, often fatal, that they received from police.

But first there was O. J. Simpson. Given that two people
were brutally murdered, it puzzles me how the low-speed chase

of Simpson in the white Bronco took on an almost farcical air, unfolding on live TV and watched by nearly one hundred million transfixed viewers. His arrest, on June 17, 1994, was followed by a "trial of the century" whose details remain too familiar to require recounting. Given the litany of misconduct by the Los Angeles police that came to light, notably the racist language and conduct of detective Mark Fuhrman, it was not entirely surprising to me that Simpson was acquitted. I recall having a polite argument with a Black friend at a dinner party after the trial was over. I thought the verdict was justified and he did not, a reversal of the opinions held by most Black people and White people. Which was more important: convicting a murderer or repudiating racist police attitudes and actions? It was not an easy call.

As we entered the twenty-first century, those who hoped race relations were improving could point to some high-profile advances, as Colin Powell and Condoleezza Rice became secretaries of state, and then a Black man was elected president, an electrifying event that allowed many Americans, metaphorically, to dust their hands and say, "Well, that's that!" Any number of commentators heralded the arrival of a "post-racial" society, a view that sounds hopelessly naive today but did not at the time. During the first decade of the 2000s, majorities of both Black people and White people consistently told Gallup pollsters they believed race relations in the country were good.

The first racially charged incident of the Obama era was a relatively tame affair, the arrest of the prominent Black scholar Henry Louis Gates Jr. at his own home in Cambridge, Massachusetts, by a White policeman responding to a 911 call from a neighbor who saw Gates and his driver forcing open his jammed front door and assumed a burglary must be underway. Obama famously convened a "beer summit" at the White House where Gates and the officer, James Crowley, made peace with each other amid widespread media coverage. As a mark of Obama's cautious approach to the subject, he commented on a "long history" of police "disproportionately" stopping Black people and Latinos but then apologized when law enforcement organizations objected. Only later, in 2012, did the president seem to find his voice, after the slaying of Trayvon Martin in Florida by a neighborhood watch volunteer. "If I had a son," Obama said wistfully, "he would look like Trayvon."

It is dogma that the sharpest recent turn in America's race relations came in Ferguson, Missouri, in 2014 with the death of Michael Brown and the rise of Black Lives Matter. Certainly it was for a great many African Americans. But I would argue that for White people, the real turning point arrived two years later, in New York City, with the police slaying of Eric Garner.

The events in Ferguson opened a lot of people's eyes to the way police in St. Louis County preyed on Black drivers, collecting fines for minor traffic infractions that fed the budgets of scores of municipalities. For the poor, the practice could be devastating. A broken taillight could trigger a cascade of fines, warrants, court dates, incarceration, probation, debt, job loss, and ultimately ruin. Profiling Black drivers and the criminalization of poverty most certainly are racist. But that part of the story emerged only gradually—in print, not on television.

Brown's death was a clarion call in the Black community, but for many White people—including me—he was not a very sympathetic figure. In his case, the salient video came from a security camera in a store, where he appeared to steal cigars and was shown shoving a clerk, hitting him in the neck. Minutes later, walking down the middle of a street, he was confronted by a police officer, Darren Wilson, driving a patrol car. Brown reached inside trying to wrest away the officer's gun and was shot in the hand. He fled, and Wilson pursued him and shot him to death. Evidence strongly suggested that Brown had been advancing on Wilson when he fired the salvo of fatal shots. I have wondered why Brown's death became such a cause célèbre in the Black community, and I suspect the reason may be found in the hours after he died rather than the minutes before. The police left Brown's body lying face down in the middle of the street for four hours, a dereliction of decency that infuriated the neighborhood and then the nation. I don't suggest Brown deserved to die, only that for me, this was not a landmark case of police misconduct.

Eric Garner's was. I was appalled at the way he died. More to the point, I could watch how he died, on an endless tape loop of video from a bystander's cell phone camera. Many images on TV are disturbing. These were obscene. I could see—and feel—the violent, heartless cruelty of a police officer clamping a choke hold on a helpless man who was not, in any real sense of the term, resisting arrest. As we could all tell, he could not breathe. That a grand jury declined to bring criminal charges against the officer, Daniel Pantaleo, struck me as a gross miscarriage of justice.

To be sure, there was abundant evidence of enduring discrimination against Black people that did not appear on a TV screen, but learning about redlining, say, did not arouse an adrenaline rush of outrage in the same way as video of police shooting a twelve-year-old boy carrying a toy pistol. No small number of White people continued to defend the police and argue that Black-on-Black homicide claimed exponentially more lives, but their ranks were shrinking, and I, for one, came to believe that distrust of the police in Black communities was entirely warranted and helped create the environment in some neighborhoods for gang warfare, drug dealing, homicide, and other pathologies of poverty that good policing is meant to fight.

Watching television is a passive activity. It troubles me that so much of my gradual evolution in thinking about race has been driven while sitting in a safe, White cocoon looking at people of a different color being killed on TV. I will make a case in a later chapter that I have also tried to do the harder work of reading the sociology and history of racism in America and the investigative journalism that undergirds the video.

Still, I was late in coming to the realization that Black people have a very real, very legitimate reason to fear their treatment at the hands of police, and it's a shame that it took pictures from a camera to bring me around. But the point, I think, is that I did come around, as have many White people. Seeing is believing. Our eyes are opening.

Martin Luther King Sr., weeping at the funeral of his wife, Alberta, in 1974.

Third-party presidential candidate George Wallace, left, and former Georgia Governor Marvin Griffin in 1968. Griffin served briefly as Wallace's running mate before Curtis LeMay replaced him.

Roy Harris.

Atlanta mayor Maynard Jackson offers reward money in the "Missing and Murdered" cases.

A search party is out looking for bodies.

Wayne Williams was charged in the Atlanta Child Murders.

District Attorney Lewis Slaton with two murder indictments of Williams.

Coretta Scott King, center, and Ralph David Abernathy, right. After her husband died, Abernathy's influence as Dr. King's top lieutenant waned dramatically.

Hosea Williams in 1980, the year he and Abernathy endorsed Ronald Reagan.

*Julian Bond, left, and
John Lewis during
their showdown for
a seat in Congress in
1986.*

Bond campaigning with Rosa Parks.

Willie Horton was made an icon of the 1988 presidential race.

Michael Dukakis was widely ridiculed as "Snoopy" after he was photographed riding in a tank.

Julian Carr.

The Confederate monument "Silent Sam."

Carl Sanders campaigning for LBJ in 1964.

Oliver Otis Howard and Chief Joseph in 1904.

President Donald Trump in Lafayette Square wielding a Bible as a prop, above, after police and military cleared out peaceful protesters, below.

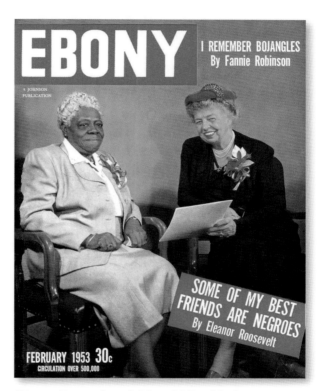

EBONY

I REMEMBER BOJANGLES
By Fannie Robinson

A JOHNSON
PUBLICATION

SOME OF MY BEST
FRIENDS ARE NEGROES
By Eleanor Roosevelt

FEBRUARY 1953 30¢
CIRCULATION OVER 500,000

Eleanor Roosevelt with Mary McLeod Bethune in 1953.

Atlanta's Freaknik in 1994.

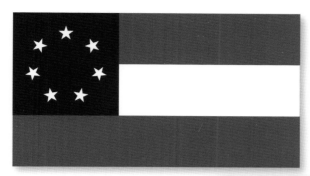

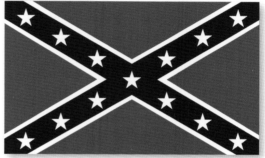

The Confederate flag, the Stars and Bars, left, was crafted to resemble the Stars and Stripes. When it led to confusion in the fog of war, Southern generals chose a battle flag with the distinctive X of the St. Andrew's cross, right, that was later appropriated by segregationists. Georgia tried an ill-fated compromise, the "place mat," below, as a state flag.

Disney's movie Song of the South *is vilified today, but actor James Baskett won an honorary Oscar for his brave performance as Uncle Remus.*

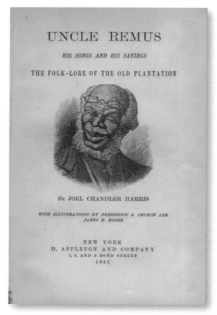

UNCLE REMUS

HIS SONGS AND HIS SAYINGS

THE FOLK-LORE OF THE OLD PLANTATION

By JOEL CHANDLER HARRIS

WITH ILLUSTRATIONS BY FREDERICK S. CHURCH AND
JAMES H. MOSER

NEW YORK
D. APPLETON AND COMPANY
1, 3, AND 5 BOND STREET
1881

Title page from the original work.

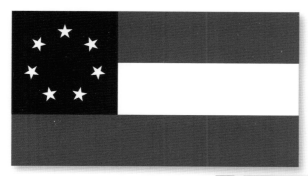

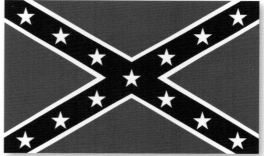

The Confederate flag, the Stars and Bars, left, was crafted to resemble the
Stars and Stripes. When it led to confusion in the fog of war, Southern
generals chose a battle flag with the distinctive X of the St. Andrew's
cross, right, that was later appropriated by segregationists. Georgia tried
an ill-fated compromise, the "place mat," below, as a state flag.

Disney's movie Song of the South *is vilified today, but actor James Baskett won an honorary Oscar for his brave performance as Uncle Remus.*

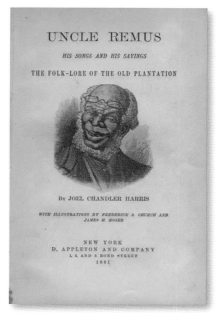

Title page from the original work.

Hosea Williams, right, led a "March for Brotherhood" in Forsyth County, Georgia, in 1987 that drew a virulent response from white supremacists, below.

Fifty years later, despite dramatic progress, there remains a great deal to protest.

Dr. King in 1963.

THE GEORGIA FLAG

In the early 1990s, after I retired from journalism to write books, I spent my workdays doing research in the reading room of the Special Collections Department in the Woodruff Library on the campus of Emory University in Atlanta.

Most of the time I labored in tranquility, but the room had an unusual feature that occasionally set off a hubbub. On the wall behind my chair, in glass cases that reached almost to the ceiling, sat Emory's impressive collection of first editions of *Gone with the Wind*, Margaret Mitchell's grand Civil War novel, translated into dozens upon dozens of languages. Every so often, groups of Japanese tourists would arrive in the reading room and erupt in loud oohs and aahs as they looked at the volumes. I was annoyed at first but then curious. What in the world did the Japanese find so remarkable about *Gone with the Wind*? And then it dawned on me. The Japanese had lost a war, as had the South. No other region of the United States had the experience of defeat in war. No other region fully comprehended what it meant. But the Japanese did, and they revered Peggy Mitchell's paean to loss.

I had a similar epiphany one evening at "Mr. C's," the legendary watering hole on Howell Mill Road in northside Atlanta. One of my regular companions there was Tom Watson Brown, a fine amateur historian and true son of the South, the great-grandson of the fiery Georgia populist Tom Watson. Without giving the matter much thought, I observed that I had a Civil War sword belonging to a Yankee great-grandfather, but knew nothing of its history or his experience, while it seemed to me that every White Southerner I knew could recite the entire military record of every ancestor who had served in the war. Why, I asked Brown, did Southerners care so much about the war when most Yankees barely cared at all? Brown started slowly at first but spoke for almost an hour, and when he was done everyone at our table was in tears. The breadth and depth of sacrifice—of loss—was vastly greater in the South than the North, so much so that it is simply unforgettable.

I touch on this question not because I mean to refight the Civil War—fear not!—but because the memory of the war is a mutable thing that has made it almost impossible for later generations to find the common ground necessary if we are ever to resolve our differences over race. Indeed, the gulf seems wider today than at any time before, with Confederate symbols throughout the South drawing fierce tribal responses. As a White man from the North, I realized early in my newspaper career that I would have to work to understand Black people. It dawned on me more gradually that I would have to work to understand *White* people as well.

Black Southerners may well greet the notion that the Confederacy suffered profound loss in the Civil War with a snort of skepticism. Or, for that matter, with fury. Perhaps no other losing side of a conflict has ever seen so much of the status quo ante restored as did the South with the collapse of Reconstruction, the imposition of Jim Crow segregation, and the US Supreme Court ruling in *Plessy v. Ferguson* that made "separate but equal" the law of the land. Black Southerners were emancipated from slavery but would have to wait a century for the rights of citizenship to be given to them, or rather wrested by them from the clenched hands of White Southerners. But I mean to argue that the losses of White Southerners were nonetheless very real, starting with more than a quarter million dead.

Let us embrace a simple premise. The soldiers who fought and died for the Confederacy were honorable young men. After reading tens of thousands of their letters and diaries, the historian James C. Davis concluded emphatically that they had "no personal interest at all" in slavery or states' rights but instead fought "because their Southern homeland was invaded and their natural instinct was to protect home and hearth." To put it more cynically, they were cannon fodder, not crusaders. The Southern politicians who seceded and formed the Confederacy were indeed motivated by a desperate wish to preserve a slave economy, but not so the young men they sent into combat. In theory, at least, the battle flag of the Confederacy should be revered as a symbol of valor.

But it has not worked out that way, and the reasons why are worth examining. When the leaders of the seceding states met in Montgomery, Alabama, in February 1861 to begin organizing the Confederacy, they disagreed about what kind of flag they should fly. One faction argued for a distinctive design that would signal a complete break with the Union. But another group, insisting that the Confederacy was just as "American" as the United States with as great a claim on the Stars and Stripes, carried the day. They created the "Stars and Bars," a flag with white stars on a blue field next to three horizontal stripes of red and white, which looked quite a bit like Old Glory. The problem was that it looked *too* much like the Stars and Stripes, sowing deadly confusion on the battlefield in the haze of war. In its place, General Beauregard and other military leaders devised a battle flag with the distinctive *X* of the St. Andrew's cross that was far easier to recognize.

That same dynamic, ease of recognition, was at work almost a century later at the dawn of the civil rights era, when the segregationists of the Deep South chose the battle flag, not the Stars and Bars, as their symbol of massive resistance. In 1948, when the Dixiecrats broke away from the Democratic Party and ran Strom Thurmond for president, their banner was the battle flag. In the 1950s, the battle flag became a craze among White Southerners, adorning neckties, bumper stickers, even beach blankets, and at times it seemed the motto of the Confederacy must have been "Fergit, hell!" rather than *Deo vindice*. In 1956, during the second year of Marvin Griffin's term as governor, the Georgia legislature changed the state flag from one based on the Stars and Bars to one incorporating the battle flag because the latter, as one supporter put it, "looked more Confederate." In sum, it was White Southerners who invested the battle flag with the symbolism that triggered protests that continue to this day.

Not all White Southerners, however, were so cavalier about the battle flag. The United Daughters of the Confederacy (UDC), which takes its history seriously, opposed changing the Georgia flag in 1956 on two grounds. First, they understood that the existing flag, adopted in 1879 and modified slightly over the years, was based on the Stars and Bars, the formal flag of the Confederacy, and was thus, by definition, more than adequately Confederate. Second, and more important, they objected to any state appropriating a sacred symbol of the "Lost Cause" for political purposes. At a time when legislation that amounted to nullification sailed routinely through the lily-white Georgia General Assembly without dissent, the bill changing the state flag very nearly failed because of the UDC.

In 1996, I published a history of modern Atlanta, *Atlanta Rising*, timed to coincide with the opening of the centennial summer Olympic Games. At the time, the state flag had become the focus of a bitter dispute along racial lines, with the St. Andrew's cross representing legacy and heritage to many White Georgians but treason and racism to most Black people. My book contained a chapter on the flag's history, including the UDC's opposition to its adoption forty years earlier. Much to my surprise, I got a telephone call shortly after publication from the head of the Georgia Division of the UDC, Sarah Dunaway, asking me if I would be willing to accept the UDC's highest academic honor, the Jefferson Davis Award, in recognition of the research I had done.

I was floored. I confess my first thought was not very noble. As a native Yankee writing about politics and history from my adopted home in Atlanta, I had absorbed a fair amount of teasing over the years—most of it good-natured, though not all—from White Southerners who wondered how I could presume to understand their region, including the Civil War and all that flowed from it. From now on, I figured, sporting the Jefferson Davis medal in my lapel like the *Légion d'honneur*, I would be immunized from any further accusations of carpetbagging. On a more serious level, I was pleased to have my research into Confederate history recognized as accurate by stewards of the subject.

The ceremony in which I was given the award was memorable. Above all else, the Daughters are genteel. They greeted my wife, Linda, and me with elaborate courtesy in a hall at Oglethorpe University in Atlanta. I had been asked to invite a few guests, and of course I made sure to include Tom Watson Brown, along with a handful of other unreconstructed friends. I was given an embarrassment of gifts—commemorative plates, Waterford crystal, a glass eagle—along with the award itself, a handsome pin with the motto "Stand Fast—Our Heritage." The UDC has a lot to answer for, having promulgated the "Lost Cause" mythology that glorified the Confederacy and glossed over its purposes. But on this one day, at least, I understood the basic human instinct to be proud of one's ancestors, not ashamed of them.

It turned out Mrs. Dunaway had a motive for conferring the Jefferson Davis Award on me. The rift over the state flag was painful for the UDC because it provoked endless attacks on a symbol of the Confederacy. Mrs. Dunaway had the simple, elegant idea of defusing the whole issue by returning to the version of the Georgia flag that had flown before 1956. Since it was modeled on the Stars and Bars, she reasoned, the old flag would honor the Confederacy, but it would remove the St. Andrew's cross that had become such a target of controversy. My research was useful to her cause, thus the award. But she also meant to recruit me for a lobbying effort at the state capitol, where legislation to change the flag had been pending, some would say festering, for several years.

One afternoon in 1997, Mrs. Dunaway and I paid a call on Tom Murphy, the speaker of the Georgia house, and rolled out her idea. It was quite a moment for me. Murphy had been one of those who teased me about being a Yankee when I covered the legislature for the *Atlanta Constitution*. Years earlier, driving through rural Georgia on a tour of the state with Murphy and his driver, a state trooper named Butch Benefield, I watched as the speaker took a bite out of a plug of tobacco, chewed it slowly, deposited the results in a Dixie cup, and then tried to take a bite out of me, accusing me of having moved south to gawk at Southerners and laugh at their backward ways. He meant to get my goat and succeeded. I lost my cool and cussed him out, and I guess I made a good case that my motives were sincere, because we got along well after that. Now I was back to see him, peddling an agenda in league with the UDC!

I would like to report that Mrs. Dunaway and I carried the day, but of course we did not. The sides had already been drawn. In the angry atmosphere prevailing at the time, not even the UDC could provide cover for removing the cross from the flag.

In 2001, Governor Roy Barnes pushed through a compromise design with five tiny versions of the state flag arrayed on a banner at the bottom—it looked like a placemat, one critic observed—and it cost him reelection at the hands of angry White "flaggers." Two years after that, the state finally adopted a flag very much like the one Mrs. Dunaway had in mind, based in part on the Stars and Bars.

The irony is plain enough. The battle flag, which should stand as a symbol of sacrifice and valor, has become as toxic as a swastika, while the Stars and Bars, representing the government of the Confederacy and an ugly ideology centered on the preservation of slavery, is bland, anodyne, and still flying. William Hartsfield, the long-serving mayor of Atlanta, liked to say that in his city the flag was "furled but not forgotten." Had it stayed that way, the battle flag might still stand for heritage and legacy. But the South—the White South—fought a second civil war nearly a century after the first one, over civil rights, and it chose the battle flag as its pennant. When it lost, the battle flag was lost as well, a casualty trampled on the ground.

JOEL CHANDLER HARRIS

A quarter century ago, when I was doing research for *Secret Formula*, my history of the Coca-Cola Company, I found myself in the cavernous, seven-acre Federal Records Center in East Point, Georgia. I was looking into old lawsuits the company filed against mom-and-pop shops and soda fountains for serving substitute syrup—the kind of thing that led to the old *Saturday Night Live* skit with John Belushi in a diner yelling, "No Coke! Pepsi!" The work was dry, literally so. I examined vial after vial of ancient, desiccated syrup, until a larger box arrived and brought a surprise: I opened it and out jumped cardboard figurines of the familiar characters from Uncle Remus—Brer Rabbit and Brer Fox and others—all drinking Coca-Cola!

I had stumbled on a long-forgotten marketing campaign from the early 1930s, in which Coca-Cola used the beloved figures created by Joel Chandler Harris for an in-store advertising promotion. Naturally I wondered why I had never seen or heard of this before. The reason was that Harris's widow and children sued the Coca-Cola Company for copyright infringement. The ensuing lawsuit dragged on for years, until a federal judge eventually ruled that all of Harris's characters were in the public domain because he had first written about them in his columns for the *Atlanta Constitution*, starting in 1876.

Even though it won the suit, the company soured on the Uncle Remus campaign and never used it. I left it out of my book. But the images stuck in my mind. In 2014, I attended a fundraiser for the Wren's Nest, the Harris house museum in the West End neighborhood of Atlanta, and got acquainted with the director, Sue Gilman. When I told her about the cardboard cutouts, she was intrigued and wanted to see them, so I made an appointment for us to visit the records center, by now moved to a new facility. The archivists there typically devote their days to the humdrum of helping amateur genealogists, so the prospect of dusting off Uncle Remus characters for an author and museum director tickled them. When we arrived, we found the figures assembled and seated comfortably on tables and file cabinets in the main storage room, like guests at a dinner party.

My involvement with the Wren's Nest coincided with my joining a discussion group in Atlanta that meets on a monthly basis to give papers. I decided that an essay on Harris's legacy might be just the ticket for my inaugural paper, so I set to work trying to decide if I thought Harris, a White man, had preserved the folklore of slaves—or had stolen it for his own purposes and profit. He was accused of doing the latter in a famous speech given by Alice Walker at the Atlanta History Center in 1981 and later summed up in her essay "The Dummy in the Window." "As far as I'm concerned," she wrote, "he stole a good part of my heritage. How did he steal it? By making me feel ashamed of it."

Is this a fair accusation? Let us start with a piece of evidence we might well call the smoking gun. When he published his first book, *Uncle Remus: His Songs and His Sayings*, in 1880, Harris wrote an introduction that described Uncle Remus, in part, as "an old Negro . . . who has nothing but pleasant memories of the discipline of slavery." This was not a slip of the tongue. In the same introduction, he challenged Harriet Beecher Stowe's portrait of slavery in *Uncle Tom's Cabin*, arguing that while it was intended as an indictment of the institution, it actually served as a "wonderful defense of slavery as it existed here in the South." So who was this man? What did he believe? Who were his characters? What were their stories? And where does his literary and cultural legacy reside today in a society still struggling mightily to come to grips with race?

Harris was born near Eatonton, Georgia, around 1846, the illegitimate son of a genteel woman who fell for an itinerant Irish charmer and found herself unwed and deserted when Harris was just an infant. Her family forgave Mary Harris and welcomed her back home, but she was reduced to working as a seamstress to make a living. Her son was a shy, redheaded stutterer, but he had a sharp mind, and he made the most of a remarkable opportunity. A man named Joseph Addison Turner owned a large plantation in Putnam County, outside Eatonton, called Turnwold. In 1862 he started a newspaper, *The Countryman*, and hired the teenaged Joel Chandler Harris to work as a printer's devil—an apprentice. Harris learned the tradecraft of journalism at Turnwold, and more important, he came of age visiting the slave quarters, absorbing the folktales of George Terrell, Old Harbert, and other venerable slaves who eventually became the composite of Uncle Remus.

Harris worked at various newspapers and eventually landed at my old employer, the *Atlanta Constitution*, where he began publishing the tales as a columnist, my old job.

What exactly was the nature of these stories? There is an entire industry of scholars studying the roots of fable and folklore, but basically the slaves at Turnwold—like slaves everywhere in the American South—told tales meant to ease the wretchedness of enslavement. The so-called trickster, as embodied in Brer Rabbit, uses his wits to outsmart bigger, stronger opponents. Sounds simple, but it isn't. I'm indebted to Bruce Bickley, Harris's most accomplished biographer, for an analysis he gave of perhaps the most famous of all Uncle Remus stories, "The Wonderful Tar-Baby Story." It is in fact a two-part tale. In the first part, Brer Fox sets a trap for Brer Rabbit: a Tar Baby. Vain, proud, demanding, Brer Rabbit falls for it, becoming increasingly furious as the Tar Baby snubs him. As Harris famously put it, "Tar-Baby ain't sayin' nothin', en Brer Fox, he lay low." Soon enough Brer Rabbit has punched the Tar Baby and is thoroughly stuck, a captive of Brer Fox.

In the book, the little White boy listening to the story asks Uncle Remus how it ends, but Remus tells him he must wait and perhaps think about it. Later, Remus recounts how Brer Fox announces he is going to build a fire and roast Brer Rabbit. Fine, says Brer Rabbit, just don't throw me in that briar patch. Or maybe I'll hang you, Brer Fox says, or maybe I'll drown you. Eventually reverse psychology works, and instead the fox throws the rabbit in the briar patch, where he escapes. Or is there more to it? Professor Bickley suggests that part one is meant as a cautionary tale for Black folk to beware the dangers of violent confrontation with the White community, no matter the provocation. What are the principal means of lynching? Burning, drowning, and hanging. By striking the Tar Baby, Brer Rabbit puts himself in immediate danger of execution. Only by using his wits and turning his adversary's strength against him does Brer Rabbit escape.

Is this reading too much into a simple tale? Hard to say. Harris has his narrator, a wise, old ex-slave, telling the tale to a young White boy who would not have understood the subtlety—but through the White boy Harris shared a vitally important message with an audience of millions, Black and White, around the globe. It is even possible that Harris passed along the tale without recognizing its full import, conveying the cautionary wisdom of Old Harbert or George Terrell directly to that wider audience.

What was Harris's purpose? What did he think of Black people? He was not out to make fun of them or their dialect, I am convinced. America in the 1800s had any number of writers and performers doing "minstrelsy," which Harris detested. His quest, in his own words, was to reproduce as accurately as possible the way slave narrators talked and to record as accurately as possible the stories they told. He was not laughing at them but with them. There is a reason Harris's Uncle Remus stories were so widely and wildly popular—why Twain admired them, why Kipling memorized vast swatches of them, why Faulkner was influenced by them, why Harris in his time was the most popular author in the world—and it's not because he was making fun of Black people. I started off thinking that Harris must have seen a father figure in Joseph Addison Turner, the plantation owner, but then I realized that Harris, literally a poor bastard, most likely identified much more closely with the slaves.

Let us stipulate for the sake of argument that Harris's purpose was benign. Did he steal stories that belonged to others? I can't give you a confident answer. I have consulted several African American scholars on this, and most will say there is nothing at all inherently wrong with the stories themselves, but they find the fact that a White man wrote them unsettling. I understand the point. Indeed, I have no quibble with anyone who is disturbed by reading Harris's Negro dialect. As for Alice Walker, she grew up in Harris's hometown, Eatonton, and had to pass every day by a restaurant on the town square that had a dummy of a servile, grinning Uncle Remus in the window—a restaurant that was for Whites only. In her short story "Elethia," she imagines breaking into the restaurant, liberating the figure, and incinerating it. I can certainly understand why she reacted as she did. But she also argues that the folklore was being passed down orally in her family and others, so Harris does not deserve credit for preserving it. I'm not sure that's so. Even if it were, that isn't the same thing as sharing the stories with a wider world. And I know for a fact that Harris did not steal the stories for a profit: one exhibit in the Coca-Cola lawsuit shows his annual income from royalties on his Uncle Remus books, and it rarely surpassed $1,000.

I was struck by Harris's insistence that a so-called other fellow residing somewhere inside him came up with the Uncle Remus stories. As a writer, I knew exactly what he was talking about. He might not have any idea what he was going to write, he said, "but when I take my pen in my hand, the rust clears away and the 'other fellow' takes charge . . . and out comes the story." He declined to refer to himself as the author of the tales, but rather the "compiler." He was, you might say, using a modern locution, channeling the voices of the slaves at Turnwold and telling their stories exactly as they told them.

Finally, then, what to make of Harris's attitude toward Black people and slavery? I am not prepared to debate anyone who believes that soft sentiment about slavery is a kiss of death, no matter how well-meaning the person who holds the view. But I mean to give Harris his day in court, if for no other reason than that these stories deserve to live on and be loved. I am indebted to a book called *American Slavery* by Peter Kolchin for some insights that I found surprising into the "peculiar institution." By the middle of the nineteenth century, even as civil war impended that would result in Emancipation, slavery was so deeply ingrained in the American South that no realistic way of undoing it short of war was imaginable. Slaves had no chance of overturning the system on their own, and thus their resistance—and their folklore—tended toward outsmarting their masters rather than rising up against them. To be clear: slaves hated being enslaved and yearned for freedom, but they had to make do in a system in which those dreams were unreachable.

Moreover, by the mid-nineteenth century, White slave owners had refined the tools they used to maintain slavery. While the punishments used to keep slaves in line could be unspeakable, it is also a fact that some plantations did not resort to corporal punishment at all—an insidious permutation, perhaps, but one that explains how Harris could have lived on a plantation without observing the forces that were at work keeping the men and women there enslaved. As Harris's biographer puts it, Turnwold "was run as a relatively benevolent and humane operation," and it is a fact that some of the slaves there remained even after they were freed.

Harris apparently was also influenced by another phenomenon, the pride taken by some slaves in the quality of their plantations and the standing of their owners. It is an uncomfortable subject, but Kolchin quotes no less an authority than Frederick Douglass that some slaves "seemed to think that the greatness of their masters was transferable to themselves." Let us consider the premise of Harris's fictional world. Uncle Remus is an ex-slave, still living on his old plantation in the latter half of the nineteenth century. In his prime, during slavery, he was the head servant, trusted enough to act as chief of staff, and in fact ran the plantation during the war when the White overseer was drafted into the Confederate Army. At the very end of the war, the scion of the family, "Mars Jeems," has returned home. Union soldiers are advancing. A sniper climbs a tree and is about to shoot Mars Jeems when Remus spots him and shoots him first. Wounded, the Yankee falls from the tree, loses an arm, but is nursed back to health, falls in love with Mars Jeems's sister, "Miss Sally," they marry, and their son is the young man who becomes Remus's audience for the tales of Brer Fox and Brer Rabbit! Seriously. This is not nonsense, though some may think so.

Harris's main character is a slave who loved the family that enslaved him, rose to a prominent position within his world, took pride in his station, realized full well what the stakes were in the Civil War, but acted to save the life of the son of the family he served, and then stayed with them after he was freed. Not terribly realistic, perhaps—but this is not the invention of some garden variety racist either. In 1904, many years after his Uncle Remus stories had made him an international celebrity, Harris wrote three essays for the *Saturday Evening Post* in which he elaborated on his view that in many plantations, the head servant was, after the master and mistress, "by all odds the most influential person on the place . . . capable of doing the honors of the household with a zest and discretion well worth witnessing . . . a gentleman from the crown of his head to the soles of his feet."

In the essays, Harris returns to the subject of *Uncle Tom's Cabin* and argues that Harriet Beecher Stowe unwittingly presented "a defense of American slavery as she found it in Kentucky." His point was that Uncle Tom, far from being a passive, submissive "old darky," was a man of tremendous character and integrity and that he was undone not by the slave system as it existed but by plot contrivances that Stowe invented for the purpose of abolitionist propaganda. Harris did not in the least want to return to slavery, but he insisted that slaves lived rich, full lives in spite of the system. He describes a plantation's "mammy" as "never anything but herself from first to last: sharp-tongued, tempestuous in her wrath, violent in her likes and dislikes, she was wholly and completely human." If you read Uncle Remus in full, you don't find an "Uncle Tom." You find a wise, wily man who imparts wisdom to a beloved child—wisdom that subverts most notions of White supremacy.

Indeed, one African American scholar, Robert Cochran, contends in an essay titled "Black Father: The Subversive Achievement of Joel Chandler Harris" that Remus is not so much a father figure to the little boy as he is a father, period, teaching the boy vital life lessons that only a Black man could understand and that his actual father is too privileged, too complacent—and too White—to grasp. By this theory, Harris knew exactly what he was doing and disguised it through trickery worthy of Brer Rabbit.

Consider this: several Uncle Remus stories are set in the home of "Miss Meadows en de gals." Who are these women? That's exactly what the little boy asks Uncle Remus when he first mentions them. And Remus answers evasively, "Don't ax me, honey. She wuz in de tale, Miss Meadows en de gals wuz, en de tale I give you like hit wer' gun to me." Hmm. Okay. Brer Rabbit likes to visit a group of women who live together, and they are a highly appreciative audience who applaud his cleverness outwitting Brer Fox; and they break into a "monstus gigglement" when they hear the story of the Tar Baby. They serve as a sort of Greek chorus— and if you read the stories closely they can be seen only as prostitutes, living in a brothel. It seems Brer Rabbit had a somewhat more interesting existence than living in a briar patch! If that isn't subversive, what is?

So are we to exonerate Harris? No. Not entirely. It is, of course, forgivable, even laudable, that a White teenager apprenticing at a plantation in the 1860s would admire and even come to love the slaves he met there and to sugarcoat the quality of their lives—especially a plantation as unusual as Turnwold. I think we can also understand Harris adopting Uncle Remus as his narrator and sharing his stories. Writing in the 1870s and 1880s, just as Reconstruction came apart, nostalgia for the old days was hardly surprising. Southern apologists had only to look at labor conditions in the North and in England during the Industrial Revolution to find conditions that seemed as appalling as slavery. Harris argued that neither race, Black nor White, was prepared to govern in the South after the collapse of the Confederacy, and perhaps he had a point.

But here's my problem: Harris held the same views in 1904— long after the establishment of Jim Crow, the disenfranchisement of Black voters, and the Supreme Court's ruling in favor of "separate but equal." In 1906, two years after Harris wrote his essays in the *Saturday Evening Post*, one year after President Theodore Roosevelt visited Atlanta and lauded Harris for promoting regional reconciliation, Atlanta was torn apart by race riots. Harris and his family actually sheltered Black neighbors on their porch and in their cookhouse. He liked Black people, wanted them to grow and develop and prosper, but he adhered to the gradualist views of Booker T. Washington, and he was blind—it seems to me, this man who wrote the tar baby story—to the crushing burden that held Black people down and literally lynched them to keep them in their place. In the *Saturday Evening Post*, Harris confronts directly the accusation that he is an apologist for slavery. "Be it so," he writes. "I never had a hand or part in slavery, but I know that in some of its aspects it was far more beautiful than any of the relations that we have between employers and the employed in this day and time."

Well, no. I met Harris's biographer, Bruce Bickley, in Harris's hometown of Eatonton in 2015, when he gave a lecture there. The audience was mostly local folks from Putnam County, all White and of a certain age. Not once but twice they asked, plaintively, what was so bad about *Song of the South*, the Disney version of Uncle Remus that had its debut in Atlanta in 1946. Why, the audience wanted to know, did Black people object so much to the movie? "Well," Professor Bickley remarked dryly, "one thing—the darkies are singing as they go to work in the fields."

Many, many people loved that movie. One of its songs, "Zip-a-Dee-Doo-Dah," won an Oscar. The Remus stories were faithfully told. James Baskett, the actor who portrayed Uncle Remus, died just two years after making the film, but not before winning an honorary Oscar. And I believe he earned it. I believe he invested that role with a dignity and grace that defies explanation. *Gone with the Wind* got away with romanticizing the Old South when it came out in 1939. Seven years later—after a world war that gave us hundreds of thousands of Black veterans with the double "V" in their windows, for victory over fascism at home and abroad—that romantic vision was untenable. Disney's real sin is that it kept re-releasing the movie in the sixties, seventies, and eighties, every time our nation had a convulsion over civil rights. I can't forgive Disney that.

So what are we to make of all this? Why does it matter today? I think it matters because it gets straight to the heart of race in America, then and now. Several years ago, I read *Go Set a Watchman*, Harper Lee's early novel, and it's dreadful, but there is one riveting scene. Scout has gone to see Calpurnia, her old maid and mammy, whose family has suffered under segregation in ways she is only beginning to fathom. Jean Louise, as Scout is now known, asks Calpurnia, "Did you hate us?" After a long moment, Calpurnia shakes her head no. Through slavery, Jim Crow, and on into today, White people have taken for granted the love that so many Black people give them in spite of it all, have been blithely unaware of the underpinnings that support White entitlement, and—this is the key—have not always recognized the bottomless reservoir of forgiveness that generation after generation of Black folk have demonstrated.

Let us give Harris the final word on this. Not long before he died, he wrote a letter to Andrew Carnegie summing up his life's work, saying "the only ambition I have ever had, the only line of policy that I have ever mapped out in my own mind . . . [is to]

smooth over and soothe and finally dissipate all ill feelings and prejudices that now exist between the races."

Harris's sin? He thought Black people could lift themselves up on their own. He could not, over a lifetime, see the chains that bound them.

JOURNEY

I first heard about Southland in the mid-1990s from my good friend Dick Williams, the host of our TV talk show and a former colleague at the newspaper. Dick's great passion in life was refereeing high school basketball games, and his vantage point on the court watching the teams gave him advance knowledge of demographic changes in the counties around Atlanta. With great glee, Dick told me about a subdivision in the southern part of DeKalb County that was caught up in a wicked irony.

In the late 1980s, developers began work on Southland, a planned community in the shadow of Stone Mountain, with its giant carving of the three horsemen of the Confederacy, Robert E. Lee, Stonewall Jackson, and Jefferson Davis. The planners gave the streets names culled from the Civil War—Antietam Drive, Manassas Run, Wilderness Trace, and Appomattox Trace. At the time, the movement to topple Confederate monuments was still a full generation in the future, and it made a certain sense to tie the neighborhood to Stone Mountain's association with the "Lost Cause."

But then a funny thing happened. DeKalb County underwent a dramatic shift in demographics, and Black families began moving into the area. By the time Southland opened, the buyers turned out to be African Americans. Suddenly there were Black families living on Civil War battle sites! After a chuckle, though, I realized that Southland was showing me something important. The families moving there were decidedly middle class, paying upward of $200,000 for their handsome new homes, playing golf on the course next door, living in what one real estate agent called "an upscale minority community." These were the success stories from the private sector: doctors and lawyers, vice presidents from Delta Air Lines, Coca-Cola, BellSouth and other businesses, and their numbers were burgeoning. In the early 1970s, when I arrived in Atlanta, it was all too easy to think that most Black people lived in public housing projects or benighted neighborhoods inside the city limits of Atlanta. Here was proof that things had changed dramatically.

Jumping ahead to 2016, the *Washington Post* took a detailed look at housing values in the aftermath of the financial meltdown of 2008 and found that Black neighborhoods had been left out of the recovery. In Southland, the *Post* reported, a home that sold for $440,900 in 2005 was resold in 2015 for only $290,000, a loss of more than a third of its value. Houses in Southland were worth about half of identical homes in northern DeKalb County, which had remained predominantly White. I have long been aware, of course, that Black families have only a fraction of the wealth of White families, a legacy not just of slavery but of more than a century of redlining and other impediments that continue to this day, accelerating the call for reparations. But I had not realized that even middle-class Black families, with

parents earning six-figure salaries, are subject to the same corrosive unfairness.

And then I found there was even more to the Southland story.
I tracked down the developer, thinking I might find a Civil War
reenactor or such, but Brad Bryant turned out to be a man of
progressive sensibilities who has devoted his career to public education. He was a bit sheepish about the street names in Southland
but noted—accurately—that if his purpose had been a pro-
Confederacy theme, he would scarcely have chosen Appomattox,
where Lee surrendered. Unlike some other developers, Bryant
and his partners had welcomed the Black families who moved
into Southland, helping them secure mortgages at Decatur Federal Savings and Loan, which was run by a liberal state legislator
named Robin Harris, the great-grandson of Joel Chandler Harris. In matters of race, I have found, tugging at threads tends to
unravel a wealth of unexpected entanglements. As chairman of
the DeKalb school board, Bryant spent years trying to desegregate the county's public schools, working closely with his Black
counterparts. None of it was enough to prevent the schools near
Southland from remaining predominantly Black—or to prevent
many Black families from moving out, in search of better schools
in other suburban counties, as the phenomenon of "Black flight"
contributed to the decline in value of Southland's homes.

For a White journalist writing about race, there are several
third rails, but perhaps none as hot as the question of Black prejudice. I got a sharp jolt in 1985 when I wrote a well-intentioned
but utterly boneheaded column about Louis Farrakhan. My thesis was that Farrakhan performed a useful service by preaching a
message of self-reliance to his Black listeners and that he gained
the standing to administer tough love by spurning the rules of

polite society. "I believe," I wrote, "that his anti-Semitism, either consciously or unconsciously, is just a device: a way of burning bridges, of cutting himself off from all conventions and niceties, of forcing himself to stand completely alone, of spitting out all the liberal mouthwash of the past several generations." It was a tool, I suggested, meant to cloak him with the authority to get through to his listeners, "and the black community is packing the house to agree with him."

I have described receiving early morning phone calls that set me back on my heels, but nothing ever rocked me the way a Jewish caller did on the day the Farrakhan column ran. I had tried to excuse anti-Semitism, and the man on the phone, weeping, reminded me in excruciating detail of the costs of doing so. A letter to the editor a few days later made the point explicitly: "The Nazis came to power that way, putting 'people in the tent' with the message of hate, selling economic benefit for all Germans and then murdering more than 9 million civilians during their reign of power." He called my column "drivel," and he was right.

I was guilty of another sin in that column, and the remarkable thing is that no one called me on it. I commended Farrakhan "for the courage to tell his followers that it is their duty to curb teenage pregnancies, black-on-black crime, poor education, drug use and unemployment." I accused other Black leaders of telling audiences that "they are victims and thus, by extension, reliant on others." Gazing back more than a third of a century, I see an earnest younger self who was blithely unaware of most of the burdens inflicted on Black people that went unaddressed at the time and remain so today. Self-reliance is fine, but who am I to deliver a sermon to African Americans? Who was I to suggest that self-reliance alone could do the job? I was wrong.

I had left the *Journal-Constitution* by the time it won a Pulitzer Prize for a series in 1988 called "The Color of Money" that laid out in stark detail the redlining that Atlanta's banks and savings and loans were imposing on Black neighborhoods, denying mortgage loans, choking off home ownership and with it the accumulation of net worth. I read the articles with keen interest—not fully grasping that the practice dated back to the 1930s, was started by the federal government during the presidency of Franklin D. Roosevelt, applied to the whole nation, and had continued almost unabated in the decades since. Nor did I guess that it would persist to this day. But I should have.

My thinking shifted further a few years later, in 1992, when I returned to CNN as a commentator covering the presidential election. I was intrigued with Bill Clinton's "Sister Souljah moment," when he denounced a hip-hop singer for an interview she gave the *Washington Post*, excusing the violence of the Rodney King riots. "I mean," she said, "if black people kill black people every day, why not have a week and kill white people?" It was a singularly ugly thing to say, and if Clinton had stumbled upon it and recoiled, his response would have been understandable. Instead, his campaign seized on the comment and saved it for the chance to make political hay. Clinton used a speech to Jesse Jackson's Rainbow Coalition to denounce Sister Souljah, saying, "If you took the words 'white' and 'black' and you reversed them, you might think David Duke was giving that speech." With his trademark calculation, Clinton accomplished his goal of distancing himself not just from a radical fringe of racial rhetoric but also from Jesse Jackson himself. He got away with it because Jackson had invited Sister Souljah to speak the night before, but the fact was that her comments were a month old, and she was a minor artist who scarcely merited such a high-profile rebuke. I thought about the criticism leveled at President Bush for the Willie Horton affair and saw a certain parallel with Clinton and Sister Souljah.

I wish I could say that I threw myself heart and soul into educating myself about race, but like most people I thought I was already educated. Over the years, I have been forgiving of native, White Southern friends who refer to the War Between the States and insist it was fought over states' rights, not slavery, because that was what they were taught in school as part of the state-sponsored curriculum, based on propaganda very successfully promoted by the United Daughters of the Confederacy peddling the myth of the "Lost Cause." It is no easy thing to overcome ideas enshrined in textbooks. The most distinguished Georgia historian of his day, E. Merton Coulter, chairman of the history department at the University of Georgia, was an unabashed apologist for the Confederacy, slavery, White supremacy, and a benighted view of Black people. "In my teaching," he once wrote, "I am still trying to reestablish the Southern Confederacy." He did not retire until 1958.

What else did I not know about? Well, for one thing, the full virulence of White supremacists. On Saturday, January 17, 1987, my old friend Hosea Williams led a "March for Brotherhood" in Forsyth County, Georgia, a suburb north of Atlanta. Civil rights marches seemed pretty passé by then, and no one expected the trouble that broke out when some four hundred counterprotesters showed up and pelted Williams and his band of fewer than a hundred marchers with rocks, mud, sticks, and racial epithets. Predictably, the ugly scene prompted a full-dress response the following Saturday, as an army of twenty thousand, Black and White, marched side by side to the county courthouse under the protection of 1,700 National Guardsmen and more than a thousand law enforcement officers. A phalanx of elected officials joined the march, and it seemed that the sort of open racism practiced by the Ku Klux Klan had been repudiated.

But I had an unsettling experience that day. Arriving at the staging area in a shopping center parking lot about a mile from the courthouse in Cumming, the county seat, I found that journalists were being herded inside a cordon of guardsmen, police, and deputy sheriffs formed to seal the marchers off from the counterprotesters. For some reason, I chose to stay outside the cordon. I think I wanted to experience the wrath and venom of the other side firsthand, and I got more than I bargained for. At the courthouse square, I was surrounded by White people consumed with fury, the knots in their mottled necks popping as they screamed at the marchers. "I guess I just wasn't prepared," I wrote later in my column, "for the numbing, sickening feeling that comes from hearing racial epithets shrieked six inches from my ear—and I mean shrieked. These people were up on their tiptoes, tearing their vocal cords, lost in a trance of pure hatred." I was never in any real danger—an assistant state attorney general recognized me and whisked me through a barricade into the cocoon inside the cordon—but I have never forgotten that moment.

Thirty years later, in August 2017, when President Donald Trump suggested a degree of moral equivalence between White nationalists and counterprotesters during a violent clash in Charlottesville, Virginia, with his now infamous claim that there were "very fine people on both sides," I thought back to my experience in Forsyth County and wondered how on earth he could possibly have said what he said.

I learned another lesson from the Forsyth march only later. The reason for the initial march lay in the county's history. In

1912, three Black men were accused of raping a White woman: one of them was lynched, and within a week, according to legend, all of the Black families in the county had been intimidated by night riders into moving out, abandoning their land without a dime of compensation. In the days after the march, legislation was introduced seeking reparations for the descendants. Objections were raised immediately, and not just by those hostile to Black causes. Cynthia Tucker, an African American columnist for the *Journal-Constitution*, warned that arranging compensation would be "awfully difficult." She explained: "Land that was seized may have been sold and resold. Are there records? Deeds? Are there black heirs? Survivors?"

Her questions turned out to be prescient. The newspaper began investigating more closely, examining deeds and other records, and engaged a professional genealogist. It found that several Black families had retained their land, while others sold, some for a profit. The findings did not gloss over the White violence of 1912 that scared the vast majority of Black residents into leaving, but they did emphasize the challenge of sorting out exactly who had lost land and might deserve compensation.

I became a convert to the idea of reparations, as I think quite a number of people did, after reading Ta-Nehisi Coates's brilliant, searing article, "The Case for Reparations," in the June 2014 issue of the *Atlantic*. I will explore the issue more fully in the next essay, but for me the bottom line has not changed very much since 1987. The theft of wealth and land that White Americans inflicted on Black Americans is very real, inarguable, and deserving of remediation at a high price. How to do so is going to tax our imaginations and patience (and wallets), but we have to try. More than a thousand Black people were living in Forsyth County in 1910, according to the US Census Bureau. Ten years later, in the next census, there were thirty. How do you compensate a family for being terrorized out of its home?

Meanwhile, my disillusionment about attaining a "color-blind" society occurred in stages. The only time I have ever held public office was my appointment to Atlanta's Urban Design Commission—the board that settles legal questions of historic preservation—by the then-mayor, Bill Campbell, in the late 1990s. I had left journalism by then, and Campbell had not yet run afoul of federal tax law, so it all seemed innocent enough when the two of us formed a friendly relationship. He gave me a signing party for my book *Atlanta Rising* at city hall in 1996 and joked of my brief mention of him, "I liked my paragraph." A dinner we had a few years later left us bruised and estranged. I told the mayor I thought welfare laws encouraged young Black women to have children out of wedlock, creating dependencies that hobbled both mother and child. "You are a racist," he responded, and that was that. We didn't speak again for years. In today's evolved atmosphere of how we talk about racial issues, I think he could have found any number of ways to question my assumptions without calling me a racist, and I am quite certain I could have expressed my views in a less offensive way—by including White unwed mothers in my criticism of welfare law, for example. I have promised not to write a book of dense sociology, so I will not attempt to litigate the issue of out-of-wedlock births here, except to note they have increased among all races.

My last lesson to mention, for now, came in the aftermath of Hurricane Katrina in 2005. Books have been written about Katrina, of course, and I will not even try to list the myriad issues they cover, but I came away with one harsh insight: you can't rebuild a slum.

For the Black residents of New Orleans, the ones who had not lifted themselves up to the middle class and moved to a Southland of their own, the flooding destroyed substandard homes they could barely afford to rent or own in the first place and could not afford once neighborhoods were rebuilt at far greater expense according to code. In the end, some one hundred thousand Black people left New Orleans for good. Not because of the explicit hate of night riders, nor the ugly epithets of White supremacists, but because an advanced nation could not figure out a way to give them back what they had lost, let alone something better.

REMEDIES

The argument that Black Americans are owed reparations—not just for slavery but for hundreds of years of patently, violently unfair treatment that has left them impoverished—is open and shut, in my view, a settled matter. But how to pay for those reparations, how to undo the damage, is a wicked, treacherous question.

It is not a new one. Every year for three decades, beginning in 1989, the late representative John Conyers, the Michigan Democrat, introduced a resolution calling for a commission to study reparations. Each year he gave it the same title, House Resolution 40, after the "forty acres and a mule" promised to freed slaves at the end of the Civil War, and each year it failed to clear committee to reach the floor for a vote. By the summer of 2020, however, amid racial tensions fanned by the death of George Floyd, the novel coronavirus, and the presidency of Donald Trump, fresh interest had been stirred and there were calls not just to study reparations but to begin awarding them.

Writing in the *New York Times* Sunday magazine, Nikole Hannah-Jones, the Pulitzer Prize–winning leader of the newspaper's 1619 Project, made a compelling case for reparations, and concluded almost breezily, "The technical details, frankly, are the easier part." Well, no, I'm afraid they aren't. Six years earlier, when Ta-Nehisi Coates revived the push for reparations in *Atlantic*, he did not dare suggest a price tag. "Perhaps," he wrote, "no number can fully capture the multi-century plunder of black people in America. Perhaps the number is so large that it can't be imagined, let alone calculated and dispensed." It would be enough, Coates said, to create the study commission that Conyers envisioned and to admit that the debt was owed.

Today the price tag is on the table, and it's enormous—some $10 trillion or more, or roughly twice the entire annual federal budget. The number comes from an influential book, *From Here to Equality*, by William A. Darity Jr. and A. Kirsten Mullen, scholars at Duke University, published in the spring of 2020, updated in a second edition in 2022, and now widely cited as the authoritative word on the subject. In its concluding chapter, the book reviews the proposals of more than a half dozen historians and economists who have attempted to calculate the amount of money that the descendants of slaves are owed for the forced, unpaid labors of their ancestors. The formulas vary, but the bottom line is shocking, ranging as high as $17 trillion. Rather than flinch at such astronomical figures, the authors write reassuringly, "The Fed certainly could manage an annual outlay of $1 to $1.5 trillion without any difficulty," adding, "and this funding mechanism would not have to affect tax rates for any American."

In my days writing a column for the *Atlanta Journal-Constitution*, I used to delight in ridiculing the wild-eyed schemes of politicians, and the notion that the Federal Reserve could print and distribute a trillion dollars a year or more for a decade without anyone paying for it—and without eventually igniting runaway inflation—would have made my day. But I've come around to the view that the cruel theft perpetrated on Black Americans is no subject for mockery—far from it—and that the enormity of it is as great as the multitrillion-dollar estimates suggest. Indeed, how can we put a price tag on a lifetime of work stolen by slavery? On a century of Jim Crow laws that stripped Black families of the ability to buy houses and create net worth? On redlining and segregated neighborhoods that persist to this day, hobbling an entire people?

Darity and Mullen put their focus on slavery and the descendants of slaves, ignoring other aspects and eras of racism. Using various formulas to estimate the value of the unpaid labor of slaves, and applying compound interest rates to carry the debt forward, they suggest a range of $5 trillion to $17 trillion owed to some forty million descendants of slaves. I expected them to urge Congress to appropriate money on behalf of Black Americans for use in combating poverty, strengthening institutions, paying off student loans, improving schools, reforming law enforcement—a menu of progressive ideas that, God willing, might work when past programs have fallen short—but no. Darity and Mullen insist that restitution should be paid directly to the descendants of slaves. *"For both symbolic and substantive reasons,"* they write (emphasis theirs), "an effective program of restitution must include direct payments to eligible recipients."

To identify these recipients, the authors recommend two tests: first, proof of at least one enslaved ancestor, and second, evidence that the recipient "self-identified" as Black at least twelve years before enactment of the legislation authorizing the reparations. It does not require much reading between the lines to recognize that these criteria are intended to prevent fraud, as millions of people line up to receive cash payments that would run into six figures. But slave genealogy is notoriously difficult to document, and racial self-identification presumably would require millions of people to retrieve their census forms to show they had checked a box for Black, Negro, or African American. The logistics are daunting, to say the least. And even if one could conjure up a foolproof method of identifying descendants of slaves, what of Black people who are *not* descendants of slaves but have nonetheless suffered the privations of racial discrimination? Barack Obama would not qualify for reparations, but his wife and daughters would. Oprah Winfrey would qualify. The children of Prince Harry would qualify. But your Somali taxi driver would not. An asylum seeker from Haiti would not.

To oversee the distribution of reparations, the authors propose the creation of a federal Reparations Advisory Board, consisting of twelve members serving staggered three-year terms, to be elected by the pool of eligible recipients, with the power to administer individual accounts and decide whether to make outright payments, hold the funds in trust, or invest in start-up businesses. These trustees would be paid a salary of $200,000 a year. A far larger National Reparations Bureau, made up of civil servants working with the General Accounting Office, would carry out the day-to-day servicing of accounts. I do not mean to be unkind, but the likelihood of bureaucratic chaos seems obvious.

What about restitution of a more modest scope, such as Georgetown University's pledge to spend $400,000 a year on programs to benefit the descendants of the 272 slaves it sold to stay solvent in the nineteenth century? Or Harvard's establishment of a $100 million endowment in 2022? Such private, individual programs are fine for assuaging guilt, Darity and Mullen write, but are woefully insufficient in scope and "cannot meet the collective national obligation." When the city of Asheville, North Carolina, approved reparations in 2020, Darity told the *New York Times* he was "deeply skeptical" that "piecemeal" spending could reach adequate levels. "Now is the time to go big," Robert Johnson, the billionaire founder of Black Entertainment Television, told CNBC, as he issued a call for $14 trillion in reparations.

Blue-ribbon commissions can be a place where ideas go to die, but in the case of reparations I believe it would make sense to create the commission that John Conyers had in mind and to see if it can conjure up a plan with a greater likelihood of success and a funding mechanism the nation can afford.

I will give Ta-Nehisi Coates the last word. Anticipating the sort of objections I have raised, he wrote in his *Atlantic* article, "The popular mocking of reparations as a hare-brained scheme authored by wild-eyed lefties and intellectually unserious black nationalists is fear masquerading as laughter." I don't think anyone is laughing these days, but there is a great deal of work—and persuasion—to be done before reparations are paid.

A close cousin of reparations is the concept of White privilege, which entered the academic lexicon in the late 1980s and has since gone mainstream. As with reparations, there is no question in my mind that White privilege is very real and that being born White in America carries with it a raft of advantages that lubricate life in ways large and small. Using humor to make the point is dangerous, of course, but I recall understanding vividly what was meant when I saw a *New Yorker* cartoon years ago in which a

Black college student insists defensively to a White classmate, "I got in here the same way you did!" And the White student, looking surprised, responds, "Your dad gave a wing to the library?" The unearned benefits of being White run a wide gamut, from enjoying various social courtesies to the comfort of knowing that a traffic stop will not end in death. In many ways, White privilege is a list of freedoms: the freedom to shop in a store without being followed by a security guard, the freedom to get approved for a mortgage, the freedom to be accepted at a college or hired for a job at equal pay, the freedom from negative assumptions based solely on the color of your skin.

Leveling the playing field seems only fair, but here, too, there are devils in the details, because "Whiteness" is more than a laundry list of forms of discrimination that ought to be ended. At the outer extremes of anti-racism, "Whiteness" is seen as a set of values—among them use of the "King's English," punctuality, delayed gratification, and "objective, rational, linear thinking," according to one training booklet cited by the *New York Times*— that are thought to disadvantage people of color. In the summer of 2020, the Smithsonian's National Museum of African American History and Culture was embarrassed by an exhibit listing supposed attributes of "Whiteness" that included hard work, self-reliance, the "nuclear" two-parent family, and a determination to "win at all costs." Under fire from conservative critics, the museum apologized and removed the graphic from its website. Suggesting that Black people are incapable of hard work and intellectual rigor is racist, pure and simple, and finding that view on display at the end of the rainbow of anti-racism is dispiriting and unacceptable.

During the summer of 2020, two books atop the bestseller lists tackled the subject of eliminating racism. Both, Robin

DiAngelo's *White Fragility* and Ibram X. Kendi's *How to Be an Anti-Racist*, struck me as problematic. DiAngelo argues that all White people are racist, and the "fragility" of her title refers to their typical wounded insistence that they are not. Her thesis reminded me a bit of a parole hearing: you must first confess guilt before becoming eligible for release; insisting on your innocence disqualifies you from consideration. I am perfectly willing to concede that most White people, me included, harbor biases we are unaware of, and likely would benefit from working to ferret them out. My difficulty is that DiAngelo insists on calling these biases racist. As she writes, "I know that because I was socialized as white in a racism-based society, I have a racist worldview, deep racial bias, racist patterns, and investments in the racist system that has elevated me." I'm sorry, but most White people simply aren't willing to flog themselves that hard. Calling someone a racist typically ends the conversation before it begins. More troubling still, DiAngelo takes aim at two "ideologies"—individualism and meritocracy—as contributing to the racial imbalance that keeps Black people down. As one Black critic noted, "Few books about race have more openly infantilized black people," portraying them as virtually helpless.

Meanwhile, Kendi's book puts forth a simple thesis that any disparity between the races is due entirely to racist policies, which must be eliminated to ensure equal outcomes. Like DiAngelo, he takes aim at a bedrock foundation of our nation, in his case capitalism, calling it a "conjoined twin" of racism, and writing, "Capitalism is essentially racist; racism is essentially capitalist." One can certainly agree that great sins have been committed in the name of capitalism, but do we really think another system would be better? In an article in *Politico*, Kendi advocated passage of a constitutional amendment that would create a federal Department of Anti-Racism with the authority to pre-clear all local, state, and federal policies "to ensure they won't yield racial inequity" and to "monitor public officials for expressions of racist ideas." The department would be staffed with "formally trained experts on racism" who would be "empowered with disciplinary tools to wield over and against policymakers and public officials who do not voluntarily change their racist policy and ideas." It is tempting, I concede, to imagine federal agents meting out punishment for politicians who utter racist sentiments or gin up racial conflict—including a certain former president of the United States—but obviously this is not a practical idea.

Another hot-button issue, critical race theory (CRT), seems to me tailor-made for misunderstanding. As of 2022, half a dozen states had banned it from their classrooms and a dozen more were in the process of doing so, largely without knowing what it is. To suggest that residual racism continues to haunt American institutions—criminal justice, employment, education, housing, and health care—is not a radical idea. But critics insist that CRT labels all White people as racists, which it does not. Reconciling these contradictory views is not on the horizon.

Having dug a shallow grave for myself as a skeptic of reparations and renouncing Whiteness, let me move on to the hottest third rail of all, the question of what responsibility, if any, the Black community bears for fixing its own problems. My short answer is, no more or less than the rest of us. Really. In the summer of 2020, as in other summers of unrest, it was impossible not to feel dismay as looting and violence broke out, leaving the night sky red with flames, with countless shops and businesses shattered, shards of glass lying in the streets like so many fingers pointing blame. As parts of Atlanta burned, I made the mistake of admonishing a Black friend that this sort of anarchy threatened to undermine the sympathy and goodwill that so many White people had felt and expressed for the Black Lives Matter movement . . . *as if it were his responsibility.* It has taken me a long time, too long, to recognize that there is no official, unified Black community that can somehow act unilaterally to undo the regrettable, criminal, fatal actions of individual Black people. My friend, I apologize. You have no greater duty to discourage rioting than I do. And I have no lesser duty than you. Your voice carries greater weight than mine, certainly, but that is not the point.

I have my fair share of White friends who utter all the weary clichés: that they never owned slaves, that slavery has been over since Emancipation, that Black-on-Black violence takes exponentially more Black lives than do the police, that Blacks should study harder, have fewer children out of wedlock, pull up their pants, that all lives matter. In keeping with my promise not to write a textbook, I will not attempt to refute each of these old saws, but I do want to follow one particular set of breadcrumbs along a path that discredits the widespread notion that some Black teenagers are socially or biologically coded for lives of violence.

In the 1980s, a crime wave swept through many American cities, widely blamed on the proliferation of crack cocaine. I recall Maynard Jackson returning to the Atlanta mayor's office in 1990 for a third term and expressing shock at the ravages of the crack epidemic in many of his city's neighborhoods. In a candid interview with the *Journal-Constitution*, he bemoaned "crime, guns, dope, lack of values, lack of direction among those who are caught up in the dope world, communities being undercut." Remarkably, he advocated the death penalty for any drug dealer who sold crack to a user who then died from an overdose or sold a gun to someone who then committed a homicide. As he put it, vividly, such perpetrators "ought to be fried."

Across the country, pressure mounted for measures to fight crime in general and crack cocaine trafficking in particular. The idea took hold that a generation of inner-city Black youth had become a menace to society, and it was not just White racists who thought so. In 1993, Jesse Jackson famously remarked to a Black audience in Chicago, "There is nothing more painful to me at this stage of my life than to walk down the street and hear footsteps and start thinking about robbery, then look around and see someone white and feel relieved." In 1994, with bipartisan support, Congress passed and President Clinton signed an omnibus crime bill that sought to put more criminals behind bars with longer sentences. The act contained a raft of provisions, from progressive to draconian, reflecting Congress's bygone willingness to compromise. There was funding for crime prevention programs, for hiring one hundred thousand new police officers, for building new prisons, inducements for states to mete out longer sentences and "three-strikes" life sentencing, a ban on assault weapons, a Violence Against Women Act meant to reduce domestic abuse, and more.

We have been arguing about the law's merits and flaws for more than a quarter century now. But there is no question that the images of violent Black men (including Willie Horton) helped fuel its passage. In 1995, the criminologist John DiIulio attended a White House dinner where he warned the Clintons about a coming generation of "super-predators"—remorseless, violent young men he characterized in apocalyptic language:

They are perfectly capable of committing the most heinous acts of physical violence for the most trivial reasons (for example, a perception of slight disrespect or the accident of being in their path). They fear neither the stigma of arrest nor the pain of imprisonment. They live by the meanest code of the meanest streets, a code that reinforces rather than restrains their violent, hair-trigger mentality. In prison or out, the things that super-predators get by their criminal behavior—sex, drugs, money—are their own immediate rewards. Nothing else matters to them. So for as long as their youthful energies hold out, they will do what comes "naturally": murder, rape, rob, assault, burglarize, deal deadly drugs, and get high.

His words had a dramatic impact. Just months later, at a campaign rally for her husband, Hillary Clinton gave a speech warning of the need to take on "super-predators" who had "no conscience, no empathy," and "bring them to heel." DiIulio was careful to include both White and Black gang members in his description of super-predators, but the lasting impression was that he and the Clintons were referring to Black youths and that they had exaggerated wildly, using the most incendiary language imaginable, creating an image that was quickly branded racist.

As it happened, the crack epidemic began to fade, largely on its own, as users gradually either died or turned against the devastating nature of crack addiction. Crime rates fell, and no new species of violent predator evolved. But the issue was far from over. In February 2016, campaigning in South Carolina before its Democratic primary, Mrs. Clinton was ambushed at a fundraiser by a Black Lives Matter activist who demanded that she answer for her "super-predators" comments two decades earlier. The intervening years had solidified the impression that the term referred exclusively to young Black men and was thus a racist libel. Mrs. Clinton tried briefly to defend herself but soon apologized. "Looking back," she said, "I shouldn't have used those words, and I wouldn't use them today." In a final irony, Donald Trump—a man who, among other things, had branded Mexicans as rapists and urged the death penalty for the Central Park Five—brought up the subject of super-predators during a presidential debate and piously chided Clinton: "I think it was a terrible thing to say."

My point? It is all too easy to think up and embrace seemingly promising cures for our nation's enduring racial ills, only to find that they do not work or they make things even worse. One of the most widely disparaged anti-crime laws ever enacted, the so-called 100-to-1 rule that equated 5 grams of crack cocaine with 500 grams of powder cocaine in setting mandatory prison sentences for drug trafficking, was considered so humdrum that it passed in Congress in 1986 with majorities of 392 to 16 in the House and 97 to 2 in the Senate. Only later did it become clear that the law worked a terrible unfairness: crack was almost entirely a Black phenomenon, while White drug users preferred powder cocaine, so that as a practical matter Black drug dealers were a hundred times more likely than their White counterparts to receive lengthy, mandatory sentences. In broader terms, that act and others encouraging tougher crime laws and longer sentences led to mass incarceration that we now realize put too many Black people behind bars for far too long.

In 2018, to his credit, President Trump signed the First Step Act, a bipartisan piece of legislation that rolled back some of the excesses in sentencing of earlier laws. Black gang violence remains a problem in many American cities, certainly, but its causes and cures are now believed to be rooted in sociology and police reform—in combating poverty and hopelessness—rather than making a crude, cruel assumption of some racial character flaw.

Hillary Clinton's mention of "super-predators" in 1996, at a time when many believed they existed, became a target twenty years later that may have kept just enough African American voters at home to cost her the presidency. The damage that can come from even the best-intentioned ideas should give us all pause in a time when the politics of race have become more adamant, more extreme, more contentious than ever. I have long been skeptical about the idea of a national Truth and Reconciliation Commission, modeled on South Africa's, that would examine our history and admit our sins over race, but I think the time may have come. It would not be a remedy, but confession is good for the soul, and more to the point we need a national accounting of what has been stolen from Black Americans.

Next, I'd like to see a commission on reparations, but I would suggest a different name: a commission on *repairs*. This may seem a slight semantic distinction, but the word reparation connotes atonement, amends, a salve for past wrongs. In the parlance of tort law, it suggests punitive damages, not actual damages, and I believe that's the reason so many White people are opposed to the idea—81 percent, according to a Gallup poll taken in 2019— because it sounds like punishment for a wrong committed by others. "Repairs," on the other hand, indicates that Black Americans continue to wear the yoke of discrimination and deserve to have the damage fixed. In an interview with the *New Yorker* in 2019, Ta-Nehisi Coates first made the point, calling for a "policy of repair," explaining, "I think what you need to do is . . . figure out what the exact axes of white supremacy are, and have been, and find out a policy to repair each one of those. In other words, this is not just a mass payment."

Fine in principle, you say, but how would it work? It would start with a reckoning of where Black Americans stand today. Campaigning in Dimondale, Michigan, in 2016, Trump memorably entreated Blacks to vote for him by saying, "You're living in poverty, your schools are no good, you have no jobs . . . what the hell do you have to lose?" A dystopian vision, but I was struck by its similarity to a bleak assessment offered by Ibram X. Kendi. The Civil Rights Act of 1964, he contends, was enacted not to benefit Black citizens but at the insistence of the State Department, whose leadership feared that overt racial discrimination was hindering the US cause in the Cold War as we vied with the Soviet Union for the allegiance of new nations emerging from colonization in Asia, Africa, and Latin America. "Racist power," Kendi writes, "started civil-rights legislation out of self-interest." Once our sphere of influence was secured in the late 1960s, he argues, the federal government turned its back on racial inequality. Indeed, in an article in the *Washington Post* in 2017, Kendi suggested that in some respects, the Civil Rights Act made racism worse, not better. "After the passage of the act," he wrote, "Americans quickly confused the death of Jim Crow with the death of racism. The result: They blamed persisting and progressing racial disparities on black inferiority."

Better, I think, to take the measure of progress. Writing in the *New York Times* in September 2020, Thomas Edsall pointed out that since 1970, the Black middle class has doubled, the number of Black people in poverty has been cut in half, the number of Black people with advanced college degrees has tripled, and the wages of Black workers have gone up dramatically. "Black America," he concluded, "is doing vastly better than it was before the advent of the civil rights movement."

(I have given Kendi a hard time in this chapter for what I consider extreme views, but one of his points lingers: it is easy to condemn a White supremacist who bombs a church in Birmingham and kills four innocent Black girls, but it is no less appalling that the infant mortality rate in that city remains three times higher for Black infants than White infants, with an estimated five hundred Black babies dying each year "because of the lack of proper food, shelter, and medical facilities." If you don't believe in environmental racism, drink the water in Flint, Michigan, in 2014 or in Jackson, Mississippi, in 2022.)

I am not qualified to advocate a detailed plan of repair, but I don't think it's a mystery what needs to be done. Reform policing. Bolster credit for Black homeowners seeking mortgages. Ease student debt. End environmental racism. Improve schools. Strengthen community programs for teens. Mentor. Tutor. Integrate.

We know what repair looks like. We know who has to do it and who should pay for it. The question is whether we will roll up our sleeves, Black and White alike, and get to work.

ACKNOWLEDGMENTS

I have inflicted these essays in draft form on scores of friends and colleagues, and their willingness to give me their time, insights, and advice is at once humbling and greatly appreciated. Three muses in particular deserve special praise: Eric Redman, my classmate at Andover, author of *The Dance of Legislation*, and head cheerleader insisting that I continue when I had doubts; Jerry Elijah Brown, PhD, journalism dean at Auburn and the University of Montana, and bona fide Southerner; George Wirth, roommate at Chapel Hill, my preacher, neighbor, and liberal theologian—these three have carried me down the field, and I thank them with all my heart.

It was harder for Black folks to read these drafts than it was for White friends, because, well, race is harder for Black people than White—if I learned anything writing this book, that was the most important lesson—and my old friends and colleagues from the AJC, Alexis Scott and Jeff Dickerson, were kind and held my hand and steadied it the whole way. Andrew Young was encouraging to me, as he has been the half century I've known him. Michael Lomax arrived back in my life and reassured me that a White man striving to gain enlightenment about race is doing something worthwhile, even if imperfectly.

My other critical readers of some or all essays, bless you: Charlie Battle, Brad Bryant, Chris Curle, Rick Detlefs, Wyche

Fowler, Peggy Galis, Jack Hardin, Tom Houck, Tom Johnson, Jim Minter, Martha Moore, Monica Pearson, Billy Peebles, John Pope, John Rivers, Jack Sibley, Jack Sineath, Tracy Thompson, Mary Chapman Webster, Betsey Weltner, and Dick Williams. For years, as my boss and then my colleague at the *Journal-Constitution*, Bill Shipp was a mentor and source of stories. The crowd at Mr. C's—Tom Watson Brown, Hal Gulliver, George Berry, Chuck Driebe, Windsor Jordan—all contributed to the education of a native Yankee into the mind of the South.

At Georgia State University, which houses the photo archives of the *Atlanta Journal-Constitution*, I thank Michelle V. Asci and Rachel Marie Senese for patiently teaching an old Luddite how to navigate their system and choose the excellent images that enhance this book. Kevin Riley, the editor of the *Journal-Constitution*, generously—and quickly—granted permission for the use of several photos from the newspaper's archives housed at Georgia State.

My experience with Forefront Books has been gratifying. Jonathan Merkh has been enthusiastic about publishing this book from the get-go. My editor, Christina Boys, improved the manuscript in countless ways with her keen eye and sound judgment. Jennifer Gingerich has shepherded the final draft with diligence and good sense. The design work has been excellent. I'm glad we all worked together.

This is the fourth book my wife, Linda, has midwifed. Her counsel is always smart and worthwhile, in this case including a very pertinent warning that a White man writing about race is treading on dangerous ground. She is quite right, but I think it's been worth the risk. I hope readers agree.

NOTES

Note to readers: Numerous citations in the first six essays are to articles in the *Atlanta Constitution* and the *Atlanta Journal*, and after their merger in 1982 in the *Atlanta Journal-Constitution*. To access the articles, go to ajc.newspapers.com, start a free trial subscription to the AJC Archives, and use key words and the date. Other newspaper abbreviations are AP: Associated Press; NYT: *New York Times*; and WP: *Washington Post*.

* * *

Author's Note: Poinsett: Wikipedia entry, city of Greenville, SC, website. A good biography of Poinsett is James Fred Rippy, *Joel R. Poinsett: Versatile American* (Durham: Duke University Press, 1935). Op-ed: Damon Young, NYT, 7/10/2020. Aisha Harris, NYT, 10/7/2019.

"Bunch": Funeral: AJC, 7/4/1974. Dawson Five: Putting the town on trial: Tom Wicker column, NYT, 8/17/1977. Poisoning dogs: Author's story, AC, 8/3/1977. Swimming pool: Author's story, AC, 8/11/1977.

Segregationists: Wallace, "career over": AJC, 1/11/1979. Visit to Dexter: WP, 3/17/1995, citing Stephen Lesher *George Wallace: American Populist*, 1994. Ford, "all family": *Orlando Sentinel*, 12/12/1993. Visit with Griffin: Author's story, AJC, 12/17/1977. Harris: Author's story, AJC, 7/2/1979. Wallace, NYT, 1/7/1979. Lewis: NYT, 9/16/1998. Sanders on Griffin: AJC, 6/14/1982. Harris obit, AJC, 1/16/1985. Bond and Harris: NYT Sunday magazine, 4/27/1969.

Atlanta Child Murders: First bodies discovered: Case chronology, AJC, 5/15/2005. Bowen Homes boiler: AC, 10/14/1980 *et seq.* Chet Fuller: AJC, 10/19/1980. Jackson re Lindbergh: AC, 11/6/1980. Jackson and pile of cash: Photo, AC, 7/17/1981. De Niro: Rosewood, p. 123. Wayne Williams summary: AC/6/22/1981. Meeting at Governor's Mansion, author column, AC, 6/28/1981. Guilty verdict: AJC, 2/28/1982. "Families . . . Still Yearning": AJ, 2/28/1982. Binder on "Nightline": 3/1/1982. Judge Smith's dissent, AC, 1/19/1984. "Dream team" appeal: AC, 11/12/1985. "Spin" theory: September 1986 issue. Mayor Bottoms: AJC, 3/22/2019. DNA test: author inquiry of Sorenson Forensics.

"Grinning, Shuffling": Abernathy and Williams endorse Reagan: AC, 10/23/1980. "These tuxedos": AJC, 11/22/1981. "Poor Ralph" column: AC, 10/21/1980. For an appreciation of Hosea Williams, AC, author's column, 4/28/1981. Williams and Lewis in Selma: Lewis tweet, 5/7/2017. My story on Jackson's inaugural: AC, 1/8/1974. Sugarman story: AC, 10/17/1974. "City in Crisis," AC, 3/23/1975 to 3/31/1975. "Grinning . . . shuffling": AC, 10/15/1981. Doug Dean quote: AC, 10/16/1981. T-shirts: AC, 10/29/1981.

The Newsroom: Tornado: AC, 3/25/1975. Reese: AC, 8/9/1974. Witherspoon's Arnold column: AC, 7/7/1979. "Largely apocryphal": AC, 7/21/1979. Witherspoon column on Shockley: AC, 7/31/1980. Shockley libel trial: Summary, AC, 9/16/1984. "I stayed mad": McCall, p. 344. Watermelon contest: McCall, p. 289. Hosea Williams encounter: McCall, p. 305. Men's room: McCall, p. 300. Conley: AJC, 2/13/1994.

Julian Bond and John Lewis: Bond and Lewis backgrounds: *Atlanta* magazine, 3/1/1990. Scheer story: Author column, AJC, 8/20/1985. Polls showed Bond lead: Author column, AJC, 5/15/1986. Elocution lessons: Author column, AJC, 4/27/1986. Lowery quote: *Atlanta*, 3/1/1990. Lewis interview: WP, 7/22/1986. Primary: AC, 8/13/1986. "Jar Wars": AJC, 9/3/1986. Alice Bond story: AJC, 4/11/1987. Young phone call to Alice Bond: AJC, 4/17/1987. Bond on "vultures": WGST transcript, 4/15/1987. Young interview from Osaka: AJC, 4/11/1987. From London: AJC, 4/18/1987. Alice Bond transcript: AJC, 6/11/1987. Barr: AJC, 6/18/1987. Bond skit on *SNL*: 4/9/1977. Bond regretted: *Hollywood Reporter*, 1/15/2014.

Presidents: "Little brown ones": AP, 8/16/1988. Bush defended: AP, 8/17/1988. Biden on Eastland: NYT, 6/19/2019. Trent Lott: Toasted Thurmond at his 100th birthday party, C-Span, 12/5/2002. Quit as party leader: NYT, 12/20/2002. Resigned from Senate: NYT, 12/18/2007. Reagan re "monkeys": *Atlantic*, 7/30/2019. Patti Davis op-ed: WP, 8/1/2019. Reagan speech at Philadelphia, MS: C-Span, 8/3/1980. Carter at Ebenezer: AC, 9/17/1980. McGrory: AC, 9/30/1980. Lewis: AC, 9/24/1980. Author's column: AC, 9/16/1980. Herbert: NYT, 11/13/2007.

Reagan in Macon: AC, 10/16/1984. Shipp column: AC, 10/17/1984. Willie Horton: NYT, 12/3/2018. *The Baltimore Sun,* 11/10/1990. "Getting Away with Murder": *Reader's Digest,* July 1988. Estrich quote: Insidepolitics.org, Candidate ads. "I would have been scared . . .": Marshall Project, 5/13/2015. Biden quote: Marshall Project, 5/13/2015.

Sanders: "not a damned fool": *TIME,* 5/7/1965. Sanders, LBJ exchange: Schenkkan, pp. 107-8. Carter campaign against Sanders: AC, Bill Shipp analysis, 7/27/1970, 11/9/1970, and interviews with author; *The New Republic,* 4/12/1975. Johnson's tape recordings: Miller Center, UVA, online, 8/25/1964 and 8/26/1964. Op-ed by author: AJC, 11/23/2014.

Silent Sam: Postcard, 6/2/1913. Wikimedia Commons. List of speakers: Programme, Wilson Library, UNC. Carr speech: Carr Papers, Wilson Library, UNC. *Alumni Review,* issue of June 1913. Wilson as racist: NYT, 11/29/2015; 11/22/2015; *Atlantic,* 11/27/2015; Berg, p. 157; *Vox,* 11/20/2015. Trotter: Berg, pp. 345-48. Harvard Law shield: NYT, 3/4/2016; Eric Redman interview. Confederate monuments: History.com, 8/11/2017. Carr on Wilson: speech text.

Reconstruction: Nez Perce War: A recent, excellent account of the Nez Perce War is Daniel Sharfstein's *Thunder in the Mountains.* I have also relied on a lengthy book proposal I prepared in 2004. "General Day After Tomorrow": Sharfstein, p. 371. Howard's early life: Carpenter, p. 3-11. "providential circumstance": Howard, p. 12. "wretched": Howard, p. 53. "wasn't yet wise enough": Howard, p. 51. Howard's calling: Howard, p. 81.

"waving handkerchiefs": Howard, p. 122. Howard and fugitive slave: New England Historical Society, undated article. "Uh, oh": *Smithsonian* magazine, 5/23/2017. Sherman: "gallant soldier": Carpenter, p. 62. Special Field Order No. 15: Foner, pp. 70-71. (Actually, while the forty acres are in the order, the mule is not, and I cannot find a written order for the loan of government mules to the freedmen.) Lincoln's "last speech": Foner, p. 74. "Hercules' task": Carpenter, p. 83. "Here's your bureau": McFeely, p. 64. Howard's letters to wife: Carpenter, p. 109. Johnson "amused": Howard, vol. 2, p. 236. "Why . . . not resign?": Howard, vol. 2, pp. 237-38. Edisto meeting: Foner, p. 160. "better for the negroes": Howard, vol. 2, p. 244.

Trump: Newspaper ad: *Daily News*, 5/1/1989. Koch and O'Connor: *Village Voice*, 4/19/1989. Trump quote, "When you guys . . .": WP, 7/28/2017. Trump on GMA: 3/17/2011. Obama produced "long-form" certificate: NYT, 4/27/2011. Correspondents dinner: C-Span. Trump on John Lewis: AJC, 1/14/2017. Trump and Cummings: *Baltimore Sun*, 7/27/2019. "Shithole countries": *Atlantic*, 1/13/2019. Trump quote in NYT: 10/16/1973, cited in *Atlantic*, June 2019. Cohen quote: *Chicago Tribune*, 2/27/2019. "Why don't they go back . . .": *Politico*, 7/14/2019. "What ensued": NYT, 6/2/2020. Trump shoves Montenegro PM: YouTube, 5/25/2017. Woodward: CBS (text from a tape recording played on CBS), 9/10/2020. Hate crimes: NYT, 11/16/2020. McWhorter: issue of November 2020. "White Christians": Jones, p. 171.

Colorblind: 20th reunion: Author column, AJC, 6/17/1986. Ray Jenkins: Obituary, WP, 10/29/2019. Studies with dolls: Legal Defense Fund, undated article, citing "Eyes on the Prize," interview with Dr. Kenneth Clark. Weltner voted against Civil Rights bill: AC, 2/11/1964. CBS poll: Cited in Roper Center report, UConn website, 7/2/2014. Atlanta school desegregation, 1961: *Atlanta Rising*, pp. 109-11. Baldwin: "I am not a ward": Baldwin, p. 75. Douglass: David Brooks column, NYT, 3/21/2017. White ancestry: *Atlanta Rising*, p. 55, citing NYT magazine, 10/13/1957. *Plessy v. Ferguson*: History.com, 10/29/2009.

Rebecca: "Grady's Gift": NYT magazine, 12/1/1991.

TV: Freaknik drew 200,000: AJC, 5/9/1994. Tucker quote: AJC, 4/22/1998. Rodney King verdict, riots: *Time*, 4/28/2022. Schuttenberg: AJC, 5/14/1992. Black/White opinions of O. J. verdict: poll, *Los Angeles Times*, 10/8/1995. Gallup polls on race: Gallup website, "Race Relations." Gates and "beer summit": NYT magazine, 2/7/2020. Obama quote: WP, 4/22/2016. White House online archive, 7/19/2013. St. Louis County municipalities: NYT, 11/14/2015, 3/4/2015. Michael Brown: AP timeline, 8/8/2019. Brown and Garner video: YouTube.

The Georgia Flag: Confederate soldiers: Davis, p. 183. Creation of "Stars and Bars," history of Georgia state flag: Allen, *Atlanta Rising*, pp. 64-68. "Place mat": AJC, 21/ 2001. Barnes defeated: AJC, 11/19/2002.

Joel Chandler Harris: Lawsuit filed: NYT, 6/20/1931. Trial record: Atlanta Federal Records Center, Ellenwood, GA. Alice Walker: *Georgia Review*, Fall 2012. Harris on "pleasant memories . . . of slavery": Harris, 1955 edition, p. xxi. Harris's early life: Bickley, p. 15 *supra*. Bickley lecture: 5/17/2015, Eatonton, GA,

Georgia Writers Museum. "other fellow": Bickley, p. 52. Turn-wold "benevolent": Bickley, p. 23. Kolchin on Douglass: Kolchin, p. 168. Harris in *Saturday Evening Post*, 1/2/1904, 1/30/1904, 2/27/1904. Cochran article: *African American Review*, Spring 2004. *Song of the South*, re-releases: Sperb, pp. 14-15. Harris letter to Carnegie: 11/2/1907, childlit.unl.edu.

Journey: Southland: AJC, 2/9/1997. Profile of family: AJC, 11/14/2010. *The Washington Post*: 5/6/2016. Brad Bryant: In addition to several candid interviews, Bryant also read most of my essays in draft form, contributing valuable observations. Farrakhan column: AJC, 11/28/1985. Letter: 12/8/1985. Sister Souljah: WP, 5/13/1992. Clinton criticism: AJC, 6/14/1992. Coulter: Jim Galloway column, AJC, 11/14/2017. Forsyth march: AJC, 1/18/1987. Second Forsyth march: AJC, 1/25/1987. Author's column: AJC, 1/27/1987. Trump on Charlottesville: CNBC, 8/15/2017. Forsyth 1912: AJC, 1/31/1987. Cynthia Tucker: AJC, 1/31/1987. Newspaper investigated: AJC, 1/28/1987; rebuttal, AJC, 7/5/1987. For a good analysis of Katrina's effect on housing in New Orleans, see FiveThirtyEight, 8/24/2015.

Remedies: Conyers: *Detroit News*, 11/1/2019. Hannah-Jones, "details . . . easier": NYT magazine, 6/30/2020. Coates: *Atlantic*, June 2014. Darity and Mullen, "The Fed certainly," p. 266. Darity and Mullen: "must include direct payments," p. 265. Darity on Asheville: NYT, 7/16/2020. Robert Johnson: CNBC, 6/1/2020. "White privilege": the phrase is attributed to Peggy McIntosh, writing in *Peace and Freedom Magazine*, July/August 1989. Training booklet: NYT, 7/15/2020. Smithsonian exhibit: WP, 7/17/2020. DiAngelo, "I have a racist worldview": DiAngelo, p.

148. Book "infantilized" blacks: John McWhorter, *Atlantic,* July 2020. "Capitalism is essentially racist": Kendi, p. 163.Kendi in *Politico,* October 2019. CRT: Brookings study, November 2021. Jackson bemoaned "crime, guns": AJC, 1/15/1992. Jesse Jackson quote: NYT, 12/12/1993. A good analysis of the 1994 crime bill: WP, 5/16/2019. Dilulio at White House: *Mother Jones,* 3/3/2016. Hillary quote: C-Span, 1/28/96. Hillary ambushed: *Salon,* 2/25/2016. Trump chided Clinton: WP, 9/26/2016. 1986 cocaine bill: WP, 7/28/2019. First Step Act: WP, 7/2/2020. 81 percent of whites oppose reparations: Gallup, 7/29/2019. Coates in *The New Yorker:* 6/10/2019 issue. Trump, "what have you got to lose?": CNN, 8/19/2016. Kendi on Civil Rights Act of 1964: WP, 7/2/2017. Edsall: NYT, 9/9/2020. Kendi on Birmingham: Kendi, p. 220, citing Kwame Ture and Charles V. Hamilton, *Black Power: The Politics of Liberation* (New York: Knopf, 2011), 4-5.

BIBLIOGRAPHY

Baldwin, James. *I Am Not Your Negro*. New York: Vintage, 2017.

Berg, A. Scott. *Wilson*. New York: Berkley Books, 2013.

Carpenter, John A. *Sword and Olive Branch*. New York: Fordham University Press, 1999.

Cox, Karen L. *Dixie's Daughters*. Gainesville: University Press of Florida, 2003.

Darity, William A. Jr. and Kirsten Mullen. *From Here to Equality: Reparations for Black Americans in the Twenty-First Century*. Chapel Hill: University of North Carolina Press, 2020.

Davis, William C. *The Cause Lost: Myths and Realities of the Confederacy*. Lawrence: University Press of Kansas, 1996.

DiAngelo, Robin. *White Fragility*. Boston: Beacon Press, 2018.

Foner, Eric. *Reconstruction: America's Unfinished Revolution, 1863–1877*. New York: Harper & Row, 1988.

Jones, Robert P. *White Too Long*. New York: Simon & Schuster, 2020.

Kendi, Ibram X. *How to Be an Anti-Racist*. New York: One World, 2019.

Kolchin, Peter. *American Slavery: 1619–1877*. New York: Hill and Wang, 2003.

Lesher, Steven. *George Wallace: American Populist*. Addison Wesley Publishing Company, Boston.

McCall, Nathan. *Makes Me Wanna Holler: A Young Black Man in America.* New York: Vintage Books, 1995.

McFeely, William S. *Yankee Stepfather.* New Haven: Yale University Press, 1968).

Rickley, R. Bruce Jr. *Joel Chandler Harris: A Biographical and Critical Study.* Athens: University of Georgia Press, 1987.

Rosewood, Jack. *Child Killer.* Columbia, South Carolina: LAK Publishing, 2019.

Schenkkan, Robert. *All the Way.* New York: Grove Press, 2014.

Sharfstein, Daniel J. *Thunder in the Mountains: Chief Joseph, Oliver Otis Howard, and the Nez Perce War.* New York: W. W. Norton, 2017.

Sperb, Jason. *Disney's Most Notorious Film: Race, Convergence, and the Hidden Histories of* Song of the South. Austin, TX: University of Texas Press, 2012.

ABOUT THE AUTHOR

Frederick Allen was an award-winning reporter and political columnist with the *Atlanta Journal-Constitution* from 1972 to 1987, when he joined CNN as chief analyst and commentator covering the 1988 presidential contest. His essays for the program *Inside Politics* earned CNN a Cable Ace Award, and Allen was cited as best political analyst by the editors of The Hotline.

Allen was a founding panelist on the *Georgia Gang*, a public affairs show on Atlanta television since 1982.

He is the author of three books. His history of the Coca-Cola Company, *Secret Formula*, was published by HarperCollins in 1994 and has been translated into seven languages. *Atlanta Rising*, a history of modern Atlanta, was published by Longstreet in 1996 and is taught at several colleges. *A Decent, Orderly Lynching*, Allen's account of the vigilantes of Montana, was published in 2004 by University of Oklahoma Press. His research into vigilante symbolism was cited by the Western History Association.

Allen graduated from Phillips Academy (Andover) and earned a bachelor of arts degree in journalism from the University of North Carolina, Chapel Hill. He and his wife, Linda, live in Atlanta and Cashiers, North Carolina.